SHAME-PROOF PARENTING:

FIND YOUR UNIQUE PARENTING VOICE, FEEL EMPOWERED, AND RAISE WHOLE, HEALTHY CHILDREN

By Mercedes Samudio, LCSW

Publishing Services provided by Paper Raven Books

Printed in the United States of America

First Printing, 2017

ISBN 978-0-9987406-0-7 (Paperback)
ISBN 978-0-9987406-1-4 (Hardback)
ISBN 978-0-9987406-2-1 (eBook)

To the woman who raised me. I am grateful for your sacrifice, and I wish you nothing but peace and blessings.

"Let all bitterness, wrath, anger, clamor, and evil speaking be put away from you, with all malice." Ephesians 4:31 (NKJV)

"Letting go gives us freedom, and freedom is the only condition for happiness. If, in our heart, we still cling to anything – anger, anxiety, or possessions – we cannot be free." Thich Nhat Hanh

CONTENTS

INTRODUCTION

Progress through something traumatic, it's not linear. It's not like we go from unhealthy to healthy, failure to success. I think it's all circular. You just come back around to the same pain, and the same loneliness. But each time you come around you're stronger from the climb.

—Glennon Doyle Melton

A letter to my 11-year-old self

I know you're totally scared right now. You're doing your best to be as good a daughter you as you can. And I know it seems like you're just a big fuck up. You didn't lie when your mom asked you to lock the front door. That damn door is so confusing sometimes. Seriously, in your heart of hearts, you thought you'd done what was asked of you.

So when the yelling and accusations start, you freeze, scrambling for a response. You locked the door. You told her so. But she didn't hear. Or she didn't want to hear. So, you stand looking up at your mom's rage-filled face, not knowing what's coming but knowing it's not going to be good. She's holding a glass tumbler and it comes hurtling towards you before you even know what's happening. It hits you right in the face and you scream. As tears start streaming down your face, you run to your room but fall in the hallway because you can't see through all the tears. When you take your hands from your face and see all the blood, you scream even louder and feel a fear you've never felt in your life. Are you going to go blind? Where is all this blood coming from? Why did she do this? All those questions circle in your mind, whirling like a vortex. And the only answer that comes to you is: you are unworthy! There is no other explanation. You suck as a human and she's right to throw the glass at you.

And the adult me remembers this incident very vividly.

Listen, I know that night was scary and it's hurt you in ways beyond the physical, in ways you still, after all these years, think can never heal. And even though you're still scared, it's okay to let me know. We can hold each other together and move forward without fighting each other. What you lived through was horrible, and it should not have happened. You're right to feel scared and you've been right to keep fighting me to make me hear you. And now, for the first time in forever, I am finally ready to hear you and not stuff you behind my protective armor. When you show up, when you're ready, I'll stop and listen. I hear you. I see you. You're loved. You're protected. She can't hurt you anymore. Fear is not a weakness. Being sensitive is not a weakness. The shame you still feel for being so hurt by this incident isn't a flaw in who you are. Your big heart was broken. And even though you strived for the next fourteen years to make your mom see you, you didn't harden your heart. You just built a brick wall.

This illustrates exactly what shame looks like for me. I've lived with these memories for years, and the shame that came with them, stuffed deep down inside me, has affected me in so many ways.

I was raised primarily by my step-grandmother and my paternal grandfather. My biological parents were never able to raise me. I've been told over my life that my biological father physically abused me. He shook me and threw me as a baby and was sent to prison for abuse. I never got to meet him. All that I know of him is from stories that others have shared with me, and those stories are usually filled with anecdotes about how his mother suffered from mental health issues (her specific diagnosis was always debated but usually centered around either schizophrenia or depression, or a combination of both), and that he messed up my biological mother by introducing her to drugs.

As I remember it, my mother never truly cared for me or my siblings. I first lived with my maternal grandmother and grandfather, until my grandmother passed away from cancer when I was four years old. Then, I lived with my grandfather and my step-grandmother, until he passed away from cancer when I was eight. Throughout that time, my biological mother visited me. I think I may have lived with her sporadically, but those memories are vague. All that I really know of my biological mother was that we look exactly alike, and that she supposedly loved me but couldn't take the stress of caring for me and my siblings. According to others, before she met my biological father, she was a smart, successful young woman on her way to that elusive happiness we all strive for.

These are the stories I was told over and over as a child—that my father led my mother to drugs, that my mother couldn't care for me, and that she was weak and unloving. It's in these stories that the concept of shame began to form in my mind. I never quite understood as a child why all these events occurred and why they all happened without my having any control over them. But without much push, I internalized each of these stories as illustrations of my unworthiness.

On top of all that, what truly laid the foundation for my deep sense of shame was my relationship with my step-grandmother. After my grandfather passed, it was predominantly up to my step-grandmother to care for me. My relationship with her became the root of what I thought of myself and how I eventually came to understand the weight of shame.

I remember when I was forced to stop calling my step-grandmother "Granny" and instead call her "Mom." I had called her "Granny" like all my cousins and her other grandkids, but after my grandfather died and she became my legal guardian, she insisted I call her "Mom." At the time, I was totally traumatized by this change. After eight years of calling her "Granny," I had no idea why she suddenly had to become "Mom." Eventually, I realized it was to distinguish her role in my life for my community. I put this together because the more we interacted with the community—church, her friends, community events, and the like—I was also told to refer to her daughters (my aunts, who were 20-30 years my senior) as my sisters. I was also not to talk about why she was caring for me. It wasn't until I was almost in my 20s that I told someone in my church, whom I'd always confided in, that my "mom" was genealogically my step-grandmother and that the ladies she constantly referred to as my sisters were my aunts. It was such a relief to take back my story and to talk openly about something that for years had me feeling like there was something wrong with my family and with the way I was raised.

Now that I'm old enough to reflect on that relationship and think about the shame that my mom (aka my step-grandmother, who henceforth will be referred as my mom) must have been enduring and feeling, I can fully appreciate that shame can be, and often is, a huge burden on the way we live our lives. Not only did she have to raise a child that was not her own, at an age where her youngest child was in her 20s, but she also had to live with the embarrassment of trying to explain that child to others. She also had to justify the caring for of this child after the tumultuous relationship she had with my paternal grandfather, which many in our community knew about. While this realization was a "hindsight is 20/20" kind of reflection, and came about after my own healing from my childhood, the effects of that shame have left a mark on how I see the world, how I see parenting, and how I understand our social consciousness of parenting.

I always knew that I had to be the good kid to help manage my mom's anger and anxiety, even though as a child I had no idea where her emotions were coming from. I believe the weight of that shame is what led her to be emotionally and verbally abusive to me. Outside of the abuse I sustained from my mom, which brought its own brand of shame my way (being called *"stupid"* or made to feel stupid is still a huge trigger that brings on intense feelings of shame for me), I also had to hide how I was actually related to her from nearly everyone in my life. This forced deception probably contributed to the depression and self-harm I experienced as a teen (and still battle with to this day). Still, I can now empathize with the shame she must have felt for her own parenting: a journey that began for her as a teen (when she had her first child at the age of thirteen) and continued with having to care for her step-grandchild.

Our society already makes parents feel ashamed when they screw up with their own small children. Grandparents who screw up their own children so much that those children are unable to parent effectively must feel that shame compounded. Add all of that to the overwhelming feelings that come with just being a parent, day-to-day, and can you understand our strained relationship? Can you see what happens to a relationship between a child and her parent when the shame builds a thicker and thicker wall between them? When you view my mom's story through the lens of how shame distorts and destroys, you can see how important it is to recognize, honor, be aware of, and reflect on the amount of shame we unconsciously place on the role of being a parent. My mom was living under multiple layers of shame, and by the time she was tasked with raising me, she was being crushed under the weight of it.

Our job is not to deny the story, but to defy the ending—to rise strong, recognize our story, and rumble with the truth until we get to a place where we think: Yes. This is what happened. This is my truth and I will choose how this story ends.

—Brené Brown

Why do I share my story with you? This is not a memoir, nor is it my life story.

I share my story because I want you to know that I understand shame. I get how debilitating it can be. I get how easily it can creep up into your self-image and consciousness. I understand that no matter how much deep breathing, meditation, and yoga poses you do, shame nags at the frayed ends of your world, threatening to strangle the life you're trying to create.

It takes us years to realize that the shame we experience as children follows us into parenthood. When we're starting to figure out how to feed, clothe, and care for these children, we find ourselves believing that we are constantly failing. And that feeling of shame comes up and begins to build a wall between us and our child.

Biological parents. Adoptive parents. Foster parents. Step parents. LGBTQIA and *trans* parents. No matter how your family has been created, the shame that wedges itself between you and your child can become a huge barrier to your parenting. No matter how many parenting books you read or Saturday seminars you go to, this unaddressed parenting shame will make even the most well-rounded parenting skill set feel almost useless and ineffective.

I know you picked up this book to gain insight into how to have a better, more functional relationship with your child. And it's completely possible for you to become both a more loving parent and a more effective parent. But it all starts with understanding shame and how it sees its way into your life and your parenting identity.

What's really preventing you from being the parent you want to be?

The basis of shame is both internal and external. When we think about shame, there are three aspects to consider: what we see, what we think, and how we process the things we think and see. In other words, shame comes from our experiential perspectives. It's difficult to see the shame others may be feeling if we have not experienced the life events they have experienced, or if we have not sufficiently developed the skill of empathy. But we also have to consider how much we are influenced by what our culture and society tell us is the norm. We have to understand that both our own internal thoughts and the external influences of the world culminate to what we feel as shame. Shame is inherently a tough thing to avoid and something that inevitably infiltrates how we live our lives.

During graduate school, I studied human behavior. It was there that I learned that humans exist in groups or clusters called "systems". Without getting bogged down in theory, the idea of a system shows us that no person lives without being a part of something bigger than his or her individual self. And, I'm not getting existential on you with this idea. As a parent, you are not just a part of your family's system. You're part of a system at your workplace, your gym, your place of worship, your kid's school, your kid's activities, and so on. Each aspect of your identity is part of a system that gives you insight into how you live and how you operate, which, as you get further into this book, you'll start to realize creates both safety and insecurity. In other words, shame resides in the familiarity of the systems you live in, as well as in those same systems' dark crevices, which we try to ignore. What I mean can be illustrated using a common expression—"two sides of the same coin". A great example of this idea is the trait of confidence: on one side, there is a positivity that makes us feel good when we accomplish something and do it well, but the other side is arrogance, which is a piece of that trait we don't like to acknowledge or admit we have. We don't tend to feel shame when we feel confident, but unfounded shame can weave itself into the other side of the coin when we feel arrogance creep its way into our consciousness. Based on the culture you live in, the arrogant side can bring more shame than you're willing to cope with.

Essentially, these systems have spoken or unspoken rules to guide our behavior, allowing us to categorize and understand one another, fairly or unfairly. Your awareness of this aspect of human behavior will help you understand how shame slithers its way into your identity as a parent.

You know something else? These systems can also create barriers to how we grow and develop. If one system fails, and if we identify strongly with that system, that part of our identity is fractured. For example, if your family system begins to be judged as dysfunctional (whether by you or someone else) and that is where much of your confidence comes from, think about the enormous effect this must have on your identity.

Essentially, when this happens, we are thrust into the chaos of that system's failure, and until it's fixed or rectified, we are in a constant struggle to reclaim our identities or fight with the arbitrarily created norms that plague that system. Throughout this book, this is what I consider to be the basis of shame.

When there is a struggle between what we want our identities to be and who we really are, we live in a dissonance that can turn into shame. For the purposes of this book, shame is defined as dissonance from our true selves caused by a piece of our identity being enmeshed in a system that is either fractured or is perceived as fractured (in this case, perception is in the eye of the holder).

To fully understand the concept of shame, we must examine the various roles and/or identities that we play in these systems. You might take on the roles of romantic partner, sibling, child, employee, employer, etc., and each of these roles has a list as long as the eye can see, on how you are supposed to behave. These roles are defined by the systems you live in and are framed by the norms in said system. And with each role in these systems, every aspect of who we are as humans has some level of stereotype or judgment, both positive and negative.

However, of all the roles we take on as a human, the role of parent is one of the most highly critiqued (by everyone from your mother-in-law to the stranger in the grocery store). And due to this role being so heavily criticized, it can feel like we are completely unprepared for the role of becoming a parent, more so than any other role in our lives.

Let me paint a picture for you:

When you're in a horrible relationship, no one tells you that it's your fault for the abuse or heartbreak. Most of the time, no matter the fault in the relationship, you will be encouraged to get out and get away from that partner to help save your sanity and happiness.

When you complain of a horrific work environment or a boss who is intolerable, very rarely does anyone guilt you into staying in that job role. Your co-workers, friends, and family will all agree that it's better for you to be unemployed than to constantly be subjected to the emotional turmoil of a toxic job. Even if it's financially not a great idea, more people will lend a hand to help you get out than will make you feel bad for having such an experience.

Even when a friendship fizzles, most people aren't going to tell you that you're a bad person for the failure of a friendship. Again, despite who's at fault in the relationship, most will say that it's not right to stay in a friendship that makes you feel horrible.

But when you're a parent and your preschooler starts biting her fellow students or your teenager gets suspended from school for his behavior? Well, everyone in your life is going to look at *you*, the parent, and wonder what you're doing wrong.

Now, I know what you're going to say: in each of the other examples, there is a choice to leave. But when you are a parent, there is no choice. You cannot walk away from a child who is causing you emotional pain and frustration.

And, guess what I to say to that...

This lack of choice is the very reason it is a senseless notion to shame parents as they navigate a lifelong relationship that must by nature have its share of ups and downs. In every other role, we support making choices to better our emotional well-being. But when it comes to the role of being a parent, we are made to feel guilty for taking time for ourselves, criticized for making parenting decisions that seem to go against established norms, and if we express any doubts about our abilities, it is seen as a cry for unsolicited and unwanted advice.

Does any of this seem lopsided to you?

Think about how shame, as we've defined it, creeps into the psyche of every parent. The shame of trying to listen to your intuition, while simultaneously trying to make sure others see you as the societal definition of a "good parent," threatens to strangle any semblance of a relationship you want with your child. And the guilt of trying to raise a healthy child in an unhealthy world, while still being an imperfect human yourself, can be such a heavy weight that you indirectly turn against yourself and your child in an effort to manage the dissonance.

As you read this, what comes up for you? I hope you're thinking, "Wow, shame is a real bitch"—because it is! Shame can be an emotional state you feel from an early age, that you're never taught how to deal with. It then shows up in your attempts to be a halfway decent parent to a child, who might grow up to be ashamed of you. It's a vicious cycle. Fortunately, we're starting to understand how to come to terms with shame and heal our relationships with ourselves and those we love. One of the best things to come out of the shame talk in recent years actually has nothing to do with parenting, but everything to do with human behavior. Dr. Brené Brown's TED talk on shame and vulnerability thrust the idea of how shame destroys lives into the limelight, and made us aware of the deep roots that shame can dig into our lives.

According to Dr. Brown, shame is "the intensely painful feeling or experience of believing that we are flawed and therefore unworthy of love and belonging—something we've experienced, done, or failed to do makes us unworthy of connection."[1] When you think of her definition and the definition that I created for this book, it's safe to say that shame is not something that helps us move forward in our lives. It's a trait that although common to humans, can be debilitating if not checked, reflected on, and healed from.

---

1   Brown, B. (2013). Shame v. Guilt—Brené Brown. Retrieved 16 December 2016, from http://brenebrown.com/2013/01/14/2013114shame-v-guilt-html/

Now, let's look at what all this means as a parent, dealing with your own shame, along with the shame heaped on you by society. Like the other roles that you have as a human, once you take on the role of parent, you get categorized and sorted into society's idea of what it means to be a parent.

How you deal with this, how you reflect on this, and how you live with this categorization all bleeds into the shame story you create for yourself as a parent, and inadvertently how you lay the foundation for the shame story your children will eventually live with.

After working with parents for over a decade as a family therapist, and now as a parent coach, I have realized that many of our shame stories begin in childhood. When I first started this journey of working with families, I had the *Pleasantville* goal of helping at least one kid not feel the way that I did when I was 18 years old. While that sentiment still shares space with my current passion, after working with so many families, I saw one common theme: in our haste to save children and keep them safe, we forget to empower and uplift the humans who have been tasked with a child's well-being. My focus shifted from child therapy, to family therapy, to parent coaching as I witnessed the healing that occurs in a family when the parents I worked with felt supported, heard, and seen, and were given the space to be authentically, imperfectly human. It was in these sessions that I witnessed the true strength of parents: not their parenting techniques, but rather their embracing of their unique humanness as they learned to give themselves and their children empathetic space to vacillate between messing up and getting it right!

One thing that I try to allow parents to do during therapy is first discover their shame story and then confront it. In my case, the shame of being raised by my step-grandmother because my substance abusing parents couldn't care for me laid the foundation for the abuse I later endured. That's what it looks like when we don't take control of our shame stories, make them our own, retell them so we can minimize the amount of pain we endured from them, and ultimately heal.

Brené Brown has talked at length about sharing your shame stories: how to do it and with whom to do it. Brown explained that if you share your shame story with the wrong person, "he or she can easily become one more piece of flying debris in your already dangerous shame storm," so it's best to make sure you have a sturdy connection with the person who has the privilege of hearing your shame story.[2] But, Brown notes, when we share our story with someone who responds with empathy, the shame we've endured cannot survive.[3] This is why parenting experts constantly tell you to find your tribe and get support. The idea of having a village to support you is a concept that we'll talk about at length later in the book. But when it comes to sharing your shame story, I'll share with you this truth: you are the author of your story, shame and all. When you hide it for fear of being found out, all it does is eat away at how you see yourself, and eventually spills out into the lives of those you care about. It is unbelievably difficult to reflect on your shame story, let alone tell anyone about it. But that's why I started the book off with my own shame story (one of them anyway)! You see, even the licensed clinician supporting you on your parenting journey has a shame story.

The most important thing to remember when managing your shame story, is to be intentional about your shame story. What does this mean? When you become aware of how taking on the role of a parent triggers your own story, you can learn how to not re-create that story for your children. The process of learning how to do this could be referred to as "shame-proofing."

A huge task, I know, but one that your life, your relationship with your child, and the overall health of your child will greatly benefit from.

---

2   Brown, B. (2013). 6 people never to trust with your secrets. The Huffington Post. Retrieved from http://www.huffingtonpost.com/2013/11/20/brene-brown-shame_n_4282679.html

3   Brown, B. (2012). Daring greatly: How the courage to be vulnerable transforms the way we live, love, parent, and lead. New York, NY: Penguin Group (USA).

How we re-create shame in our children

So, how do we recreate our shame when we're raising our kids? There are five ways that parents recreate shame for their children:

1. Ignoring your own healing

2. Fearing your own story

3. Allowing societal norms to dictate who you are

4. Allowing your defense mechanisms to drive your decisions

5. Trying to shield your children from life based on your own experiences

Let's go through them, one-by-one.

Ignoring your own healing

The stigma of not being emotionally and mentally healthy is the thief of healing. When we try to tell ourselves that we are "alright," we are dismissing our need to heal from our negative experiences. The shame of being perceived as emotionally unsound, and therefore unable to raise "healthy" children, perpetuates our refusal to seek help and begin the healing process. But a spotless health record is an illusion. Just as we cannot go throughout life without having a cold or getting physical ailments, we cannot go through life without having some emotional and mental roadblocks. Not every emotional issue requires a trip to the institution or a prescription for medication. But thanks to society's misguided understanding of mental health, most of us believe that not being emotionally perfect is an issue. That distorted perception creates a barrier to parents working on their own healing, and brings those unhealed experiences to the decisions they make for their children.

Fearing your own story

This one I can relate to in so many ways. Growing up in a situation where I was told to lie about our family story led me to believe that something was wrong with my family and with me. I lived with that truth for so long that even now I forget to talk about my actual siblings, and I cringe when someone mentions the real genealogy of a family member. It's a fear that many parents, especially parents who have had trauma in their childhoods, live with daily. What if my kids find out about who I used to be? What parts of my story are kosher enough to discuss with them? And at what age? What will I do if a family member decides to share a piece of my story without my permission? These anxieties are both valid/legitimate and debilitating. When we are in constant fear of our story, we will do what we can to get away from it, thus stopping us from reflecting upon and growing from that story, and keeping us from developing empathy for our children when they encounter similar experiences. Essentially, this creates a shame bubble that we give to our children whenever they come anywhere near the part of our story that we're fearful of.

Allowing societal norms to dictate who you are

Another way we inadvertently introduce shame into our children's lives is by letting cultural norms tell us how to be a parent. Especially in Western cultures, there is a desire to find the "good parent" handbook, something so elusive and ever-changing that any parent who is struggling to keep up will be left in the dust far quicker than you can even imagine. The hard part, however, is that the people around you, and who are part of your parenting unit, also prescribe to these societal notions and will not miss an opportunity to let you know how you're failing. This constant barrage of what you're supposed to do can cloud your judgment and give you a complex about who you are supposed to be and how your child is supposed to act. The shame that comes from this subtly infiltrates your family. Since you believe the societal terms of being a parent, it's not until your child is struggling to keep up with these notions that you realize they might not be as useful as you once thought.

Allowing your defense mechanisms to drive your decisions

This works in line with the first and the second: when you ignore your healing, and fear your story, you inevitably create defenses to keep you safe from your past experiences. These defenses can feel almost natural and innate, and since their main function is to protect you from everything that looks like your past, even if it's your child, they can be very hard to detect and reflect on. The unfortunate aspect of this is that your child has no idea why your yelling, ignoring, punishing, and shutting down behaviors are directed toward them. They internalize it as their fault and begin to build a shame story based on your defenses, which they didn't create.

Trying to shield your children from life based on your own experiences

Since we all have instant information, now that the internet is literally at our fingertips, we can be overly focused on keeping our children safe in ways that stop them from developing resilience and coping skills. When we fail to reflect on what truly scares us and makes us anxious, we indirectly live out those issues vicariously through our children. We lash out, anticipating that they will mess up because we think we know the trajectory of their decisions (although we assume that trajectory based on our own history), and we set up walls to keep them safe because we think the world will tear them up the way it did us. And all throughout, we are helping them create shame stories that are based on our realities, as opposed to their own experiences.

One way that I encourage parents to manage these pitfalls, of creating shame for their child, is to develop a skill I call reflective parenting.

Sometimes we're so concerned about giving our children what we never had growing up, we neglect to give them what we did have growing up.

—James Dobson

The case for reflective parenting

Reflective parenting is when you take time to think about how your parents and/or caregivers raised you, what they gave you and didn't give you (materialistic and not), and how their parenting affected you. While this can be a painful experience for some, the idea is not to get deep, but to take a reflective look at what your parents did, so that you can pull from the positives of your upbringing instead of solely running from the negatives. There is no right or wrong way to do reflective parenting, since the goal is to give space to the memories of your upbringing in a non-judgmental, self-empathetic way. The goal is not to forgive your parents or even worry about whether you're doing it like them. The bigger idea here is a play on that adage, "I'll never do what my parents did to me." What I teach my private clients, and what I'll share with you here is this: to make changes in the way we see and do things, we have to be aware of how those thoughts and perspectives were created. To simply say you're not going to do like your parents, without reflectively understanding what led to their decisions, is an ill-fated attempt. Without reflection, you're bound to fall into the same pitfalls as your parents, because you didn't fully understand why they raised you as they did.

One of the parents that I worked with once shared this with me:

> I think I'm jealous of the way my kids are being raised. I had the goal of raising my child in a home filled with love and support so that they'd feel safe enough to explore the world. I'm jealous because I never had someone love me enough to commit to raising me like that.

As she talked, she began to cry. And her story is one that is all too familiar in the work I do with parents. I bet there has been a time when you too felt jealous of your child for having a better life than you did, or even a bit resentful that the life you're providing your child is better than the one you had as a child.

Let me share with you two ways that you can begin to bring more reflection into your parenting. The bigger picture that I'm painting for you will help you to see that the more reflective you are in your parenting, the more effective you can be at shame-proofing your parenting (which is why you picked up the book in the first place, right?!).

Bringing in reflective parenting

The two tools I encourage you to use in being reflective will empower you to be grateful for the parenting you received, or grieve for the childhood that you didn't get. Both are integral to creating a space for your child that will allow them both to be joyful and to grieve when they are older. It creates a space that says having feelings about my childhood experiences is okay.

1. Feel Joy

No matter how you have processed your childhood, there are things that you can think back on and have joy about. The weekends with cousins, Christmas morning, family trips, birthday surprises: some of us have more and some have fewer, but these are the things that bring us joy when we think back on our childhood. For me, it was weekends with my cousins. We all lived within ten miles of one another growing up, and I remember long weekends of video game playing, movie watching, getting into trouble, and fantasy playing hijinks. Those are times that I cherish more as I get older because they were great memories to hold onto despite some of the not so great memories in my childhood. So, how can you create a space for your child to do the same thing?

- Let your child choose what memories are theirs. Don't try to force the trip to the zoo as their most fun birthday, but rather always ask them what their favorite moments are. It might surprise you that some of the most mundane things are the memories that your child may end up holding dear.

- Share with your child your favorite childhood memories. But make sure to leave it at that. Don't add that although you had a great Christmas one year, it was ruined by a drunk father. Let them see that you can find joy in your childhood as well.

2. Feel Grief

This one is sometimes the easiest for parents to do. We are always able to bring up the pain of the past, whether it's healthy or not. But for the sake of your child, make sure that you grieve for your childhood in a healthy way. This is important in helping them one day be able to grieve for the things that have (and possibly will) hurt them as they grow older. It's okay to be angry for not getting the toys, the love, or the support that you needed when you were younger. And it's okay to want to give your child all that you didn't have. But remember this simple fact: your child will not see the world the same as you, because you raised them in an environment that was different from how you were raised. For example, the survival skills you had by the age of 13 won't manifest in your child, because they were not raised in the same home you were raised in. For me, I have to understand that my knack for determining threat in my environment will not be a trait my children develop, because I will strive to create a safe zone for them where being hyper-vigilant is not necessary.

Give yourself time to reflect on what I just said. It's okay to be upset by this realization at first. Your child will not know how to survive the things you did or learn to do things at the age you learned to do them, because you'll raise them in a different environment. In so many ways that is a good thing. But in other ways, it becomes your responsibility to teach them what you learned in a safer, healthier way than how you had to learn them. Let's check into how that may look:

- Teach rather than scold. Yes, you knew how to wash clothes by age 11 because you were the oldest sibling. Well, your only child has never had that experience. Cut them some slack while at the same time honoring your skills at that age by showing them the ropes.

- Share your story. I love storytelling and think that it is the best way to heal and grow. If you're having a hard time relating to your child because they are in another mind space than you were at that age, make a story about it and share it with your child. Share how you had to do things at their age, and how it helped you learn specific skills. Then, let them share their story with you about who they are at the same age. You might be surprised at how they see their world versus how you saw yours at that time in your life.

The understanding here is that your children will have both joy and grief over your parenting, no matter how much we attempt to do it differently than our parents. The simple fact is that perspective plays a huge role in how we process life experiences.

Here's the truth when it comes to both sharing stories and being reflective: we have our own shame stories. The hard part isn't acknowledging this; it's actually acknowledging that this is part of human life. Your children are not immune to creating shame and experiencing guilt for themselves, no matter how safe you make their environment.

We watch our kids create their own shame stories for the years they live with us, and we have to learn how to shame-proof ourselves and our families so that these stories do not consume us, but rather helps us heal, grow, and learn.

Along the lines of creating shame stories for our children, there is another aspect of parenting that culture seems to be a part of: the difference in how we see men and women in their parenting identity. This divide is something that I will explore a bit later in the book, but I wanted to introduce the concept here to get your wheels turning about how we can sometimes inadvertently teach our children this gender divide, without even thinking about it.

The Dad Effect

The Dad Effect is the experience a child receives from having male energy be a part of their caregiving unit. Gender stereotypes aside, men generally have a specific energy that is different from a woman's, and that's a positive piece for your child's development. Whether this male energy comes from a biological father or not, a child can benefit from knowing how that energy fits into their overall experience in the world.

The Dad Effect is a specific experience that moms often overlook as they attempt to manage their own shame and parental guilt. The need to control what Dad does, the desire to be right and for Dad to be wrong, and the ability to shake a dad's confidence as he makes decisions for his children, all come from the shame that we throw at parents.

It seems odd, doesn't it, that the same culture that criticizes dads for not being in their child's lives and not helping moms raise healthy girls and healthy boys, is the same culture that thinks of dads as mere babysitters, laughs at dads with "go ask mom jokes," and refuses to add baby stations in men's restrooms. It's a double standard working against dads. They can't be nurturing, they can't be home makers, they can't possibly know how to care for their children without mom's input, and they can't be quick on their feet when something happens. The Dad Effect is an integral piece of shame-proofing parents that I will delve into later in the book. But I wanted to bring it up here so that as you read further you're able to think about how we treat dads in this parent shaming culture, and how detrimental that treatment can be for the overall health of families.

Social media and shame

One of the things that I have learned as a consumer of our social-media-obsessed world, and as a parent coach who hears parents constantly compare themselves to others, is that we are always a post away from feeling horrible about our decisions and envious of others' seemingly perfect lives. To think that our children are immune to this tragedy as well, is preposterous and detrimental to helping them learn to manage their own shame.

> *One reason we struggle with insecurity: we're comparing our behind the scenes to everyone else's highlight reel.*
>
> —*Steven Furtick*

We lament the demons of the internet while still being controlled by it. We worry that our children are addicted to it while simultaneously plastering their first day of school pictures on our feeds to show that we are great parents. We judge our children for wanting more followers and likes or shares, while feeling "less than" when no one notices our hard-fought image collages of that wonderful vacation we uploaded last night. It's all a part of the lie, that our kids are so different than us, and that we have to control them. Parents fail to realize that the truth of human behavior is that we are all the same; we are just on different parts of our journey.

As parents, you'll get to watch your child create their shame stories on Facebook and YouTube and SnapChat and whatever other social media app arises from the ashes of our voyeuristic culture. But what you won't get to do is shield them from it. You get to see your child fall for the same popularity contests you fell for, without being able to shield them from the desire to be seen. You get to use your wisdom from your years of navigating the pitfalls of growing up, just as your child walks into the very things you thought you could shield them from.

We blame the internet for many of our problems, but hasn't it always been this way? I remember, as a girl, being the best subject for my mom's friends. Whenever they would come over, my mom would brag and rave about how amazing her daughter was and what amazing things I was doing. She'd call me out of my room to have me stand there awkwardly as she bragged and her friends cooed their applause and accolades at me. It was embarrassing, and it made me feel horrible to know that she would praise me in public but shame me in private.

Do you have any of those memories? Did your parents ever do that to you? Or was it the opposite, that your parents berated you in public and tried to assure you they were proud of you when no one was around?

Either way, with the advent of social media, we have taken that age-old experience of bragging about our kids to the virtual realm. Social media has created a space for us to portray a part of our parenting identity that we get to control. We can't control the meltdowns or the unwanted behavior, but we can wrangle our kids into the perfect selfie at the beach or the happy family photo at the amusement park. We can post statuses about our child's first day of school, shoot a video of their winning shot during a game, or post a screenshot of their heartfelt messages to us. It's a very validating notion for you if you're struggling to find positives in your parenting identity. And of course, this is true for the opposite side of parenting too: posting updates of our children's recent tantrums, sharing images of a child who's crying for no apparent reason, which are all attempts to validate the difficult experience of raising kids. There is no judgment here from my end, but the point of bringing your attention to this phenomena rests in the hypocrisy of shielding our children from the dangers of the very thing we use to get support.

Addressing the cost in labeling

Another aspect of how we create shame stories for ourselves and our children is the use of labels. We hear labels from our earliest days as children. Sometimes they're positive, sometimes they're well-intentioned, and sometimes they're destructive. But if we don't reflect on the labels that have been applied to us throughout our lives, we'll never fully understand our shame stories.

When I was growing up, lots of labels got thrown my way that didn't help me flourish. I heard words and phrases like, "You're stupid," "You're so lazy," "You're not like him or her," "You're too short," "You need braces," and other not so nice things. I internalized a lot of it, and it led me to have low self-esteem, to feel alone, and to hurt myself physically and emotionally. These negative labels were ones that I carried into my young adulthood, and it took a long time to really get them out of my head and heart.

On the other hand, I was also told, "You're so smart," "You're a class act," "You're such a good girl," and "You're so nice." As I got older and started to fail, I felt scared that those labels would be taken away from me, so I kept my failures and disappointments to myself. I wanted people to see me as a smart, nice, good girl whom they could rely on to make the right decisions. These positive labels ended up being just as detrimental to my self-image as the negative ones, because of my desperation to hold on to them.

The reason labels are so strong and stick so much is because we internalize what people we care about say to us. As children, we look to our caregivers for guidance and support in developing a sense of who we are. But a lot of the time, a flippant remark from a caregiver can latch itself onto a child and stick with them for years. When we label a child as lazy, stupid, fat, skinny, smart, cute, or anything else, we are essentially telling them how to think about themselves. In our haste to make a child understand who they are, we sometimes forget that they are trying to process a lot of information about their world, while also developing a self-image that they will carry for the rest of their life.

But we must use labels in our everyday world to help identify and categorize things. When labels are used effectively, they can help your child develop a strong sense of self. When labels are used to nurture a child, they can give the child the confidence to break through barriers and change those labels as they develop. And when we use labels as ways to guide our children, we can give them the space to explore who they are.

There are two main ways that I encourage you to look at the labels you are using for your children, and to rethink the ones you have used in the past:

1. Talk about who your child thinks they are

When kids are young, they have such a sense of wonderment with the world that they will tell you that they are Spider-man one day and that they are a cowboy the next. But as they get older and more influenced by their world, that sense of wonder goes away. I challenge you to encourage the lost sense of wonderment in your child again by talking to them about who they think they are. For example, ask your child questions such as:

- If you could be anyone in the world, who would you be?
- If you could change your name for one day, what name would you choose?
- Let's say you have an infinite amount of money. How would you spend it?
- If you could give yourself any title, what title would you give yourself?

These questions tell you a lot about your child's thoughts about themselves and give you more information about how to help them develop a healthy self-image. For example, I like to call myself Batman because I lost my biological parents when I was young, and now I work as a parent coach to support and empower parents. Didn't that give you a great picture of who I am (and my obsession with Batman)?

2. Challenge labels placed on your child

Let's face it—no matter how you choose to see your children, someone else will have their own opinions. And since you cannot change others' views or stop them from sharing those views with you and your child, I challenge you to reframe them for your child. If a teacher tells you your child is lazy, you can offer to sit down together to brainstorm possible reasons for this perspective and to find solutions. If someone in your community says your child is bossy, you could reframe by saying your child is a leader. This carries even more weight when you can use these reframes at home with your child. When you feel the urge to say that your child is bad, you can instead say that they have a different perspective on what they should be doing right now. Reframing is not dismissing the issue. It is putting it in another perspective so that your child internalizes not the negative label, but rather potential solutions. Additionally, when you challenge labels, it changes the way you see a behavior or issue and gives you space to find more effective solutions for your child.

Parent shaming begins at conception

We've established that you bring your own shame story into parenting, and the moment people know you're pregnant, countless new doorways open for shame to enter into your developing story—often for the most ridiculous choices. Let me share with you a story from an expecting mother who wanted to share her story with me, named Belle. And, I think you'll find the sudden shame she had thrust upon her pretty surprising.

The beginning days, weeks and in all honesty, months of this pregnancy were rough. I couldn't eat anything. I couldn't tolerate the scent of anything. Everything changed so drastically as I went from being not pregnant to pregnant; the world was spinning beneath me. I did my best to take everything moment to moment, breathing through the unknown and discomfort.

In those early days, the worst part was being unable to eat anything (well, I could eat bread and cheese, neither of which are staples in my usual diet). As someone who is in active recovery from anorexia, the relationship I had cultivated and had with food these days was one I thrived in and deeply cherished. Food brought me not only the fuel to function and exercise daily, it also brought me pleasure. When the pleasure in eating disappeared, it left me devastated. I cried often as I attempted to find something I could stomach. I would ask my body every few hours what it could eat and yet, the joy and pleasure in eating was missing.

We are delivering at a birthing center and part of their program and model is to meet in a group every trimester for support and community. I looked forward to our first group because I was hopeful I wouldn't be alone in this. We went around the room and shared our current experience in our first trimester. I shared a story from the day prior, relating to my non-stop nausea. My husband and I had gone to Costco to grab a few things and he was starving. We went to get him a snack and I knew I needed to eat something, but nothing sounded appetizing. I settled on a hot dog. I used to eat them with ketchup, mustard, and onions. I was hopeful it would taste good. I took one bite and was immediately repulsed. I spit out the bite and cried. And cried. And cried. Then I ate the crust from my husband's pizza.

It felt good to share this with someone other than my twin since no one else knew, other than the people at the birthing center, I was pregnant at the time. I was hopeful that I would hear a "me too." Instead, I was met with immediate shame. The mama to my left jumped right in to tell me that I could have purchased the nitrate-free hot dogs that are safe for baby, that I needed to stay the heck away from the hot-dogs made in house by Costco.

My heart hurt. I felt so shamed and yet couldn't say anything in response. She hadn't heard me at all. She didn't hear my sadness, devastation, or my hunger. She hadn't heard that I had spit out the bite I had taken. Instead, she felt the need to tell me what I should have done, how I needed to protect my baby from the danger of nitrates.

In my shame, I was left with no words. I was completely blindsided by this, especially as it was just minutes after we as a group had established boundaries to support us all in this process group. I had believed it was safe to share vulnerability and realized that couldn't have been further from the truth. I began to question myself and buy into the belief that I was a bad mom for thinking the hot dog was even an option to consider eating. I was saddened and I struggled with staying present for the remainder of the group.

It took me several days to verbalize what I had experienced. Thankfully, I could recognize this for what it was: parent shaming. This world of parenthood is a tricky place to be. There are endless opinions and schools of thoughts. It seems everyone has the answer and if you choose to do anything different, you are wrong, bad, and going to royally screw up your child.

My first experience of parent shaming was painful. I know this won't be the first time I will face and endure the shaming by others on my parenting choices. Yet, what I do know and will keep close to my heart is this: their shaming has nothing to do with me and everything to do with them. I will stand by my truth, trusting that the choices my husband and I make are right for us and our child. Most importantly, I will think twice before ever sharing advice with other parents so as to minimize my own shaming of parents.

With stories like that, is it any wonder that shame wedges its way in between ourselves and our children? Belle already struggled with food issues, and then to be berated for a food choice with her in-utero child, you can bet that she'll be tempted to bring shame-based decisions to a toddler who is a picky eater.

When others shame us, and we allow that shame to affect us, we're also allowing the shame to affect the choices we make as parents. It is imperative to remember that we all shine and grow when we embrace both our shame stories, as well as our success stories.

The Shame Iceberg

I want to introduce you to the Shame Iceberg. Many child therapy strategies and interventions make good use of the iceberg metaphor to help parents understand what they are seeing in their child's behaviors. When we look at the behavior iceberg, it shows us that our child's behaviors are much like an iceberg: the ice we see at the top of the water represents the external behaviors, what we see in our children daily, while the ice beneath the water represents the internal processes—including the feelings, thoughts, events, perceptions, and concepts a child internalizes—that feed into the external behaviors. In this metaphor, the ice above the water is nothing compared to the larger mass beneath the water, which is what makes icebergs so dangerous in the sea.

The Shame Iceberg, as it's applied to shame-proof parenting, is similar. But instead of the ice representing your child's behaviors, the ice above the water represents the behaviors a parent presents to the world, whereas the ice beneath the water depicts parent's feelings, thoughts, shame, and processes that feed into the parent's external behaviors. The shame iceberg doesn't necessarily have to denote only negative experiences, but the iceberg is a great illustration of how easy it is for shame to weave its way into your life and shade even your most simple behaviors and processes.

What the Shame Iceberg also shows us is how we become convinced that we need parenting strategies, parenting classes, parenting books, and all other logically reasonable ways to manage our child's behaviors, in order to mediate the barriers that shame produces for us all. An important piece of the shame iceberg is that variation between the external reasons we choose to seek support and the internal (sometimes unconscious) drives that we have to manage the bigger shame in our parenting lives. When we seek support to only manage the external factors that express themselves—like searching for advice in parenting books—we leave out how important our internal processes are for our overall well-being. I created the Shame Iceberg to give you an external space to reflect on your own inner struggles so you can see how your feelings affect your behaviors, and how sometimes shame influences the feelings you have.

Conclusion

The meat of this book will support you in identifying your shame and where it originates, defining what shame-proofing your parenting looks like, and helping you to be a great guide for teaching your children how to do the same. The result will be a healing relationship between you and your child, one that enables you to truly address behavioral issues at their root cause, whether your child is a toddler, a tween, a teenager, or a young adult.

To get to that glorious relationship, we'll start with the parenting techniques you've been told you need. We'll check out why you feel you need them, set up your confidence and intuition, and get you ready to see the truth: you've never really needed parenting strategies at all.

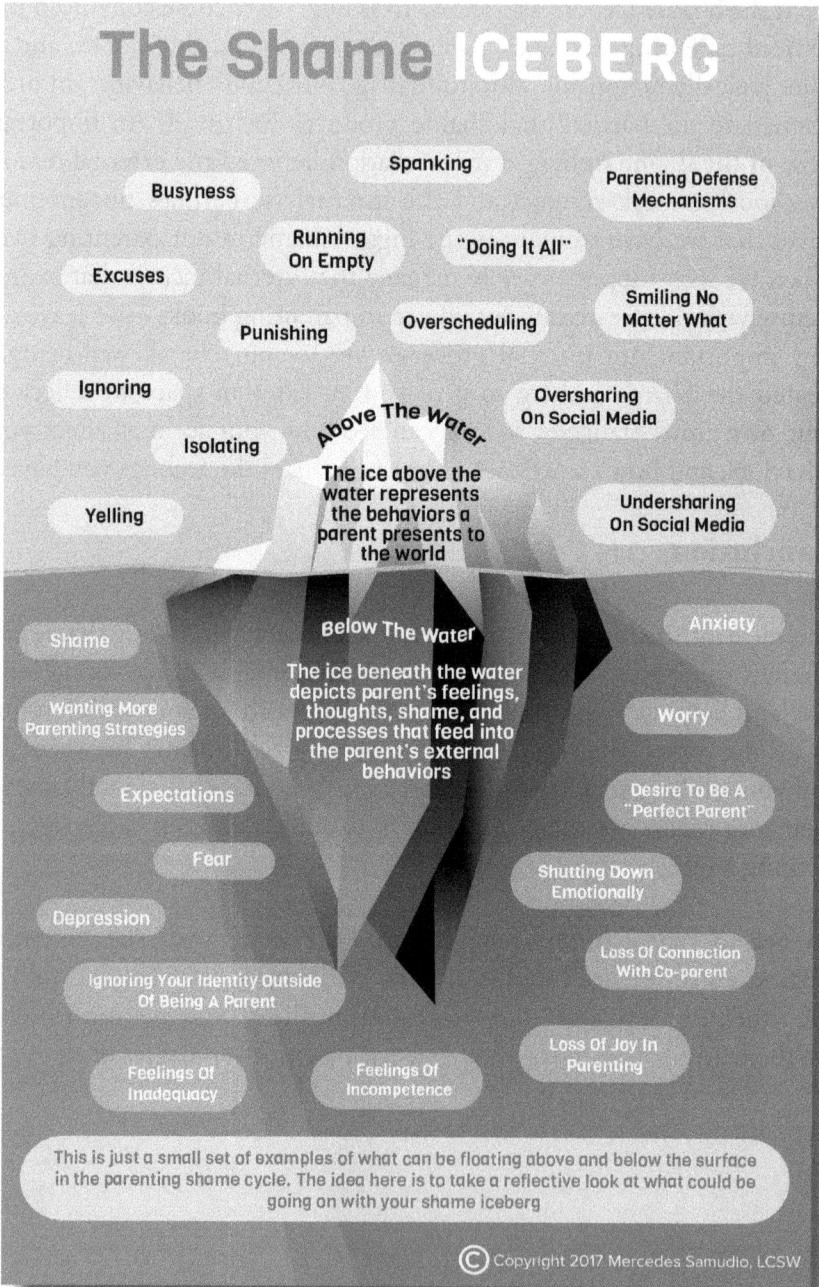

The Shame ICEBERG

Busyness

Spanking

Parenting Defense Mechanisms

Running On Empty

"Doing It All"

Excuses

Smiling No Matter What

Punishing

Overscheduling

Ignoring

Oversharing On Social Media

Isolating

Above The Water

The ice above the water represents the behaviors a parent presents to the world

Yelling

Undersharing On Social Media

Below The Water

The ice beneath the water depicts parent's feelings, thoughts, shame, and processes that feed into the parent's external behaviors

Anxiety

Shame

Wanting More Parenting Strategies

Worry

Expectations

Desire To Be A "Perfect Parent"

Fear

Shutting Down Emotionally

Depression

Loss Of Connection With Co-parent

Ignoring Your Identity Outside Of Being A Parent

Loss Of Joy In Parenting

Feelings Of Inadequacy

Feelings Of Incompetence

This is just a small set of examples of what can be floating above and below the surface in the parenting shame cycle. The idea here is to take a reflective look at what could be going on with your shame iceberg

© Copyright 2017. Mercedes Samudio, LCSW.

THE PARENTING STYLE GIMMICK

Trust the wait. Embrace the uncertainty. Enjoy the beauty of becoming. When nothing is certain, anything is possible.

—Mandy Hale

Let's be honest. When we encounter someone who is an asshole, we immediately wonder if their parents spoiled them, or if their childhood made them into the adult jerk they are today.

And as parents, we then want to know the "right way" to not raise an asshole. When our toddler starts biting or spitting, we think, "Oh no, I'm raising an asshole." So, we start looking for the quickest, easiest solution to the behavior problem.

I remember a conversation I had with a colleague about how parents raise their children. She mentioned that one of her biggest pet peeves was when she sees parents not correcting their child's "bad" behavior. She griped that when parents don't manage that behavior with their child, that child grows up to be an asshole, and then other people have to deal with that asshole adult. And don't we all share similar sentiments, often without even realizing it? When we see a parent in public fail to stop their child from having a tantrum, or see a child yelling angrily at their parent, we begin to think about what that parent's strategies are and how they let their child do this to them. It's a judgment call that we have all made, including me. And it's a judgment call someone has probably made about you.

As I reframed for this colleague, that when we see this behavior we are usually seeing a slice of a bigger picture between this child and that parent, I realized that we are accustomed to believing that it's solely up to a parent to make a perfect child. When we allow this thinking to permeate our consciousness, it's no wonder parents struggle to combat shame as they try to raise a child who hopefully won't have a tantrum, or display similar behaviors, in public. In a roundabout way, the judgments we place on other parents create impossible expectations for our own parenting, and that creates this vicious cycle of needing to control our children so they don't become the assholes we shame other parents for creating.

When you think about it like this, that's a real Jedi mind trick we play on ourselves, isn't it?

As I work with parents, I realize that we create for ourselves a desperate need for parenting gimmicks that confine our parenting to a strict set of impossible rules. Our desire to not create assholes, paired with the shame that society creates, mixed with the woes of our own childhoods, prompt us to seek out parenting strategies that suck us into this idea that if we find the "right" set of parenting skills, we will avoid raising unhealthy children who become unhealthy adults.

We are all looking for the magical solution to quell the external behaviors that are symptoms of more internal processes. When you look at it like that, it's no wonder parents spin around and around, trying to maintain their sanity as they pressure themselves into the notion that one solution will save their families.

Before I jump into this critique of the parenting world, let me start by saying that it's much better to have a plan than to not have one. When you pick up a parenting book, or save that article with the newest parenting research, you are doing what we as humans love to do: plan, research, and attempt to execute. This cycle is why the self-help world is booming. It's why your social media feeds are filled to the brim with how XYZ solution will cure all and make you gazillions of dollars in ABC steps. And it's certainly why we believe that no matter how deep the issues go, if we just follow the steps, we'll see results.

I've been a victim of this cycle in almost every step of my life, too. I'm not immune to the idea that there must be a simpler way to end the pressure and turmoil of managing my life.

To the parent who has sat in too many meetings about their child, there must be some truth to this. To the mom who is tired of cancelling plans because she knows her child's behavior will be a catastrophe, there has to be something that will work. To the dad who is really struggling to be present after a long day and just wants to hang out with his kids without having to yell, there has to be a magic formula that ends the chaos. In these parents' lives, reading that they can stop yelling, be peaceful, and reach a sort of parenting Zen in their journey to raise healthy kids, is a fantasy that they're willing to spend their hard earned cash on. And for every parent who hears about this fantastical solution, there is a parenting gimmick for you.

When I started the journey to saving lives through social work, back in 2003, I fell prey to those gimmicks, too. I thought that armed with my bachelor's in psychology and my knowledge of child development, I would rush into a family's home, talk them through their barriers, and voila, they would be on the path to healing and healthiness. It was a dream I had for my own story, too.

I wanted to come back to my mom and siblings with theories and interventions that showed my family that we didn't have to wallow in dysfunction, that we could be healthy together. And all would be well.

So, imagine my chagrin when I realized that people just don't work like that. I didn't work like that, to be honest. For all the knowledge I had, I was still reeling from my childhood and trying to make sense of the hand I was dealt, while watching friends who had seemingly whole families be able to thrive in their lives.

So, if I didn't miraculously heal from my knowledge of all the mental health issues that plague humans, why would my bringing that knowledge to others heal them miraculously? At that time in my life, that answer was elusive.

Many parents live with a parallel experience. They read all the latest parenting blogs, commiserate over all the funny memes that pass on their social media feeds, spend countless hours buying parenting books that collect dust on their shelves, and when they read the books, spend even more hours trying to figure out why it's not working for their family. They sit flabbergasted that with all their savvy, their determination, their resolve to make changes, they are still sometimes at square one with their parenting and their relationship with their children.

So many parents are still looking for that one gimmick that will finally work. But let me shine a light on the shadows that can be cast on you as a parent: it's all a gimmick.

Why parenting experts create gimmicks and why parents love them

Here's the rub: it's not a bad thing that there is no magical solution. These parenting experts, gurus, and professionals are not selling you snake oil. Trust me. They believe, generally speaking, everything that I shared with you above. And some even know that the real work will take place once you put their book down and start connecting with your child.

So, why would a parenting expert write a book about a gimmick, then? Why create a false sense of hope for parents, knowing that you'll have to do deeper work to make it all a reality?

The truth is that many, not all, parenting experts have to package their voice and message in a way that creates some urgency for you. It's well-meaning packaging, but it's still marketing. It's done to get their message heard and remembered, and to sell books (or classes, or programs, or whatever else they're promoting).

But before you jump down my throat contesting that it helped you, and before you state that I'm doing the same thing here with this book, let me clarify some things.

My fellow parenting colleagues have realized one thing that parents haven't realized, yet. That one thing is, that when we are in pain, we seek help. When we feel ashamed and anxious, we look for answers. And when we're at the end of our rope, we're most likely to hear the solutions given to us, even if they were offered to us earlier.

As a parent coach, I often get parents who come to me after trying every strategy they were aware of. Therapy. Play therapy. Attachment parenting. Conscious parenting. Figuring out their kids' "type." Free range parenting. Helicopter parenting. And every other parenting type you could imagine. The elusive magical cure wasn't found in those strategies, and so these parents found me and asked, "What's wrong with us?"

In the message of this book, I aim to get rid of the shame the parenting world has indirectly created. I don't judge or bash any of my cohorts for the parenting strategies and research they've presented. But I do reframe a lot of parents' worries that there is something wrong with their parenting because those strategies didn't work.

What's clear to me (even as I attempt to brand my parent coaching with my own "End Parent Shaming" concept) is that while all these solutions look good on the surface, unless you are truly attuned to your family's core issues and barriers, no solution will work. No matter how researched it is. No matter how popular the strategy is. No matter how world-renowned the parenting expert appears. These parenting gimmicks are best executed—and can produce valuable results—with a foundation of connection and understanding that only comes from peeling back the layers of shame that have accumulated in your parenting and in your family.

Let's talk about how a parenting gimmick might be showing up in how you're raising your children.

Anytime a new parenting style comes out, you gravitate towards it because maybe this will be the thing that "fixes" all your problems. You're at the end of your rope because X behavior cannot continue happening. By the time your parenting gets to this point, I can almost guarantee that reflection and awareness have been smothered by guilt, shame, disappointment, frustration, and sadness. This leads you to genuinely, wholeheartedly believe that this parenting expert has the right idea. And, in that instance, you're neither right nor wrong about that. Desperation and fatigue create distorted images for us all. You are like the thirsty desert hiker who could swear he saw water, but when he blinked it was gone. This parenting mirage is exactly where you need to be. You can almost see a happy, functional relationship with your child on the horizon, and that mirage will give you the courage to take the steps that will create change.

But wouldn't it be a wonderful thing to have the level of reflection and awareness to set your family up for success before it all goes to hell?

Well, welcome to Human Behavior 101, folks. That's just not how we work as humans. We don't walk around thinking about the pain of parenting until it hits us personally. When we worry about raising assholes, it's not always from our own experiences or even our own perspectives. It's usually from what society has told us makes an asshole. And in that fear, we are led to believe that there is a way to not create an asshole.

Yes, having a game plan (even a gimmicky game plan) will help you start down the right path towards restoring your relationship with your child. The truth is that we all start out as parents with a plan that has been embedded in us from our culture, our societal norms, our fantasies about what our families will look like, our expectations for our parenting, and what the current trend says are the best traits a human should have. When we start to feel like we're "failing" at that plan, this is exactly when we get desperate and seek out the gimmicks, but even those gimmicks are a course correction that we hope will create that picture-perfect family.

Our difficulty in being fully present with whatever is going on with our children is fueled by the mismatch between our Snapshot child, who exists only in our imagination, and the real flesh-and-blood one in front of us.

—Susan Stiffelman

Take a minute to reflect on the parenting strategies that most resonate for you. When you think about the human you're raising, what traits do you envision her having? Who do you see in your perspective? What flaws do you envision him having? Who do you see her becoming? Now, think about the strategies that you have in your tool box already for how you're parenting that vision, not the actual child you have, but the vision of the child you have.

If you took a moment to do that quick reflection, what came up for you? Honestly and genuinely, did your vision link up to the strategies that you're using (or attempting to use)?

For instance, you may think you're raising a generous child, but when your child is in a play group with other children and doesn't want to share, you defend her right to play by herself.

Or maybe you felt that you would have a child who would be extra close to you, and then when he was born, you realized that you had a more self-reliant child who didn't need you as much as you'd hoped.

It's interesting that, even as logical as we are about being open to what we get and loving whom we're blessed with, we still feel disappointed when our child does not live up to how we envisioned him or her. Or even still, you may think that you have a pretty resilient kid who can withstand bullying, but finding out that they are the victim of a group of peers can feel very frustrating.

But whether you did the visualization or not, I'll be frank with you: the parenting strategies you're coveting are usually geared towards the child you envision and not so much the child you have. And if we go deeper, the parenting strategies that you want so badly to implement most likely fall into two categories: the ones you wish your parents had used to raise you, or the ones you guilt yourself into believing you must use to be as different from your parents as you can possibly be.

The vision that you have for your child is not a good or bad thing. It's part of our existence as humans to dream about the unknown and hope for the best, no matter what. I mean, the whole new age, Law of Attraction world is built on the belief that if you think of something and feel *into* it deeply enough, it will materialize in your life. There is nothing predictable about raising children, but that still doesn't stop us from hoping and praying we will have a child who we can connect with, and one that will allow us to be our best selves.

But, the complications with these visions we have for our children come only when we are inflexible, and when we hold fast to them as a means to validate our parenting identities. This is when the visions you've created can become a barrier to your child's development and a hindrance in your identity as a parent. If the vision of your child does not pan out the way you thought it would, you can find yourself in a downward spiral of shame that keeps you from being the parent you thought you'd be. What I share with my parents is this simple but hard to swallow truth: your child is a separate human who will come with her own unique characteristics, and while these traits are supported by your parenting, they are not solely the result of your parenting. When you begin to see you and your child as separate beings, no matter how many people tell you she is your physical twin in appearance and mannerisms, you will not only begin to see your value in your parenting identity outside of your child's successes, but you will have given your child space to be a human, separate from the confinement of your goals, dreams, and aspirations.

And that, my friend, leads us right back to the matter at hand: that guilt and shame are a plague on your parenting journey. Not only do these two fiends distort the actual humans you have in your care, but they distort the perspective you have of yourself. They take hostage the vision you had for your family and force you to believe that you need those parenting strategies so desperately.

You don't need gimmicks. You don't need parenting books. You need a healthy, honest relationship between yourself and your child.

The reality of the parent-child relationship is that it is, and will be, just as messy as every other relationship you have. That's the hardest truth that I will share with my parents, because it unravels a fantasy that many parents have about the role they take on as caregivers for their children.

Many parents want to either do better than their parents, be like their parents, or heal their childhood wounds while raising their children. While there's nothing wrong with any of this, and it's something that I actually encourage parents to reflect on, you can hit a wall with these as your foundations for your parenting role.

The sole reason these foundations produce a barrier for you and your child, is because they don't leave any space for your child to be different than you; they don't leave any space for your child to be uniquely human. Without even being intentional about it, your own fantasies about parenting place impossible expectations on your child. He will never be able to fulfill those fantasies or those expectations, because their foundation and inception have nothing to do with him, as a person.

When you look at this perspective, you can see how this internal battle you carry as a parent—to raise a healthy human in the present while trying to heal from your own past—can make you think that you need to use parenting strategies to get your child in line with what you think your child is supposed to be, and what they are supposed to do.

Let's reframe that pressure not to raise an asshole, because your child is absolutely going to have a little bit of asshole in her overall personality, and you won't have done anything to facilitate that. It's one of the aspects of being human that I want to normalize for you: we cannot be perfect all the time, nor can we always give the right response when we are triggered by something in our environment. Yes, that's right. Even with all the tools and strategies, our human inclination to react will sometimes trump what we logically know is the right thing to do. It's the nature of being human that when we are triggered, we don't always handle things the right way. So, it's safe to say that we all have a little bit of asshole in us.

That's not to say that we don't need to help our children manage their emotions, become emotionally literate, and develop skills to navigate the treacherous waters of human interactions. What parents can focus on is raising someone who knows how to repair a ruptured relationship. You want to raise the person who can say, "I'm so sorry, I was an asshole to you. Let's repair our relationship."

But, when a child is reprimanded for being a human, we teach him that to have those emotions in the first place is wrong. We create a false expectation of what it means to be an emotionally charged person. Your child begins to build up a wall between themselves and you, because he spends most of his time defending himself and why he had those negative emotions to begin with, but he spends no time reflecting on how he'd like to repair the relationship and make a better decision next time.

Children have never been very good at listening to their elders, but they have never failed to imitate them.

—James Baldwin

As part of looking for the most effective and useful parenting strategies, I encourage you to reframe the goals you have for your child and for yourself. You will never be a perfect person, and neither will your child. Think of how we label specific behaviors as "disrespectful," when it's really just your child's normal reaction in an attempt to manage her emotions. And while we'll get into how to manage the feelings that are triggered in you when your child is learning to develop emotional intelligence, right now, let's acknowledge that becoming human is a journey, even for you, and that there is no gimmick, strategy, or short cut to walking down that path.

As we raise humans with our impossible standards and with a collection of gimmicks, we set them up to have unrealistic expectations of themselves, which can lead to more guilt and shame, and in turn, create a cycle of shame that carries them into their parenting roles.

Conclusion

The bottom line is this: no matter what parenting strategy or style you choose to use, be sure to set realistic expectations for both you and your child. You are the most important force in their life. And no matter what you bring to this role, you are the right person for the job. The parenting strategies are there as support, but they cannot take the place of your relationship with your child!

HOW YOU CAN LEARN TO STOP WORRYING AND LOVE YOUR UNIQUE PARENTING STYLE

At the end of the day, you are your wisest advisor.

—Marie Forleo

Now that we can see more clearly how shame enters our relationship with our children, and how sometimes the parenting strategies we cling to add another layer of disconnect, let's lay the foundation for how to shame-proof your parenting. Ultimately, I want you to get better at trusting yourself, your humanness, and your child's unique journey.

The best parenting strategy is one you've had all along

Intuition has become a buzzword in our collective psyche. Its overuse has almost diminished its value in people who already were on the fence about it. The simple fact that it *is* being talked about so much allows those who don't believe the space to ignore these concepts and predicate all their ideas on pure logic and analytical prowess. Or, they have tried the intuitive crap, and haven't quite gotten it, so assumed it wasn't for them.

The unfortunate part of all this is that intuition is not strictly new age. Intuition is something that is inherent in all humans. But thanks to the gimmicky nature of making money off hot topics, you're probably calling BS on this.

Let me check you into the reality of intuition.

Have you ever felt like you knew exactly what was going to happen before it happened? Have you ever had a dream that came true? Have you ever felt that something happened with your child at school only to get a voicemail from the school confirming that something did happen that day? Or have you ever known exactly what happened between your two children even while they are both trying to tell you their version of the story?

The thing about intuition is that it's there, but it's been stolen from us by the same thing that I've been preaching about throughout this book: the shame thief. We feel weird for knowing things and are constantly made to feel like we are wacky or quirky for having intuitive hunches. Or, we feel there is no logical evidence to prove how we know this, so we ignore or hide the knowledge to keep from looking like a weirdo. Or, even more common, we fear the unknown, and that uncertainty can cause us to ignore our intuition. When we ignore our intuition, we ignore our gut instincts, oftentimes to the chagrin of our own lives. We miss opportunities, we kick ourselves for not acting on what we felt, and we shake our heads over the knowledge we had, because we couldn't figure out how to explain how we knew it.

But the ultimate reasoning for me emphasizing how important it is to trust your intuition in a book about parent shaming, is that not trusting your gut is what leads you to create barriers with your child and within your parenting.

I cannot tell you how many times a parent has told me exactly what they knew their child needed, or exactly what their child was feeling, or exactly why their child made that decision. They state, when I ask about how they feel about the solutions for their child's behaviors, that they knew all their child needed was attention, or love, or connection, or space to be themselves. But can you guess what stops them from trusting that intuition?

The idea that they are being too permissive; the notion that their child won't learn a lesson without punishment; the desire to stymie their contemporaries' judgment of what type of parent they are; or the need to not raise a spoiled brat who doesn't realize that the world won't cater to them.

In a parent educator training session (specifically, Nonviolent Child Raising) I did a few years back, the facilitator, Ruth Beaglehole, talked about how we have to stop perpetuating the idea that parents need to toughen children up for the real world, but rather we need to be the cushion they return to from the harshness of the real world. Another perspective of this same idea is a common quote by Frederick Douglass: "It is easier to build strong children than to repair strong men." The overarching idea is that parents may think tough love (here defined as "the fact of deliberately not showing too much kindness to a person who has a problem so that the person will start to solve their own problem"[4]) is going to help make their child more resilient, but that is not always the case. Why, you ask?

The relationship with your child is one built on an emotional foundation where your child relies on you not solely for their physical needs being met, but also for their emotional needs. The relationship works two ways: your child fulfills some emotional needs for you as well. This foundation is why using tough love backfires for parents. If your child is looking to you for emotional stability and assurance, and you turn it off to teach a lesson, they actually don't learn that they need to harden up; they learn that they are not worthy of obtaining that emotional assurance. This begins the development of defense mechanisms that grow as they get older and get further confirmation from you that they don't deserve this emotional safety, and eventually turn into the defense mechanisms that you probably use now as a parent. Now, the interesting thing is that from your perspective as a parent, you're not hoping that they develop defense mechanisms from this tough love approach. You

---

4   Tough love meaning in the Cambridge English dictionary. Cambridge University Press, 2017. Retrieved from http://dictionary.cambridge.org/dictionary/english/tough-love

genuinely want them to build a thick skin, learn from their mistakes, and build more resilience. However, we learn those skills from having someone consistently providing emotional safety and assurance. With a foundation of emotional assurance and safety, we feel more confident to test relationships and experiences, and it's in those instances that resilience is developed.

> *Speak to your children as if they are the wisest, kindest, most beautiful and magical humans on earth, for what they believe is what they will become.*
>
> *–Brooke Hampton*

Another analogy for this is that parents are the safety net to their child's trapeze artist. As a trapeze artist learns new death-defying tricks, there is always a safety net there to catch them if they miss the swinging bar or their partner's hands. That's you, the safety net. Your child will mess up and they will make mistakes. Your safety net of emotional stability and assurance ensures that these missteps don't metaphorically injure or kill an aspect of their identity. But once the trapeze artist has a better hold of the trick, the safety net is removed and they can add that trick to their routine. That's what happens for your child. Once they get better at managing that issue, they no longer need you to be that safety net, and they can take that skill with them as they navigate their world.

The notion that they need to toughen up their children for real life, combined with their tendency to ignore intuitive hunches, is what I hear from so many parents and confirms how detrimental shaming parents can be. It leads them to bypass the gut reactions they have for supporting their child's healing and leads them to make decisions that are not always congruent with their true intentions for their family.

A mom of a fourteen-month-old son disclosed to me that the more she watched her son, the more she felt in her gut that something was wrong with him. But not in a bad way, in a way that only a mother could know. However, with this being her first son and not really knowing what she should be looking for, she did the one thing that most moms in the 21st century do: she researched the symptoms she was witnessing. She found that her son may have a sensory processing disorder. And although she felt sad about finding this out, she was relieved that there was an explanation for the symptoms she was experiencing with her son. So, of course, feeling relieved, she started to talk to her family about the symptoms she was seeing and the way these symptoms were affecting her relationship with her son—and in turn her feelings as a mom. But as she began to explain her concerns and observations to her mother, mother-in-law, and other family members she was met with dismissals and deflection. Apparently, her intuition was wrong and "this sweet little boy" couldn't have any issues at all. This dismissal made this mom feel small, made her distrust her intuition, and made her think twice about asking for support from people whom she thought were on her side. As she bounced the idea of seeking an assessment for her son, she felt overwhelmed with all the decisions she'd have to make alone; not to mention the stress of being able to care for a child who may be experiencing sensory processing issues. It wasn't until she broke down and cried after weeks of feeling lost without support, that her mother finally agreed that she should take her son in for an assessment. As this mother explained this to me, she told me that she finally understood what it felt like to be shamed. She stated that even if she was wrong about the sensory processing issues, it felt so lonely to know in her gut that this may be the issue with her son and to not have any support at all to follow up on her research.

Learning to trust your intuition can feel a bit silly, especially if you have become accustomed to ignoring it for so long. Here are some amazingly simple ways to tap back into your intuition that are not necessarily all *woo-woo*:

1. Get good at listening to your body

One of the biggest barriers to hearing your intuition is not taking care of your body. When your body is filled with aches, pains, unhealthy foods, and other ailments, it can be hard to distinguish between a stomach cramp and an intuitive nudge that is resonating from the pit of your stomach. Recognizing where your intuition presents itself is going to be integral in learning to listen to it, so get your body in healthy form. There is a myriad of ways to do this that don't include diets or excessive exercise regimens. You can get a physical to see where your pains are originating. You can drink more water to help with digestion. You could make sure to eat at least three times a day instead of forgetting meals. (That one's really for me, too). But most importantly, get to know your body and what it's trying to tell you. On that same note, learn to trust what your body is telling you. No matter how much of a super parent you think you are, our bodies don't run off imaginary super serum. You need rest, you need food, you need time to stop. Trust that when you are feeling not like yourself, that your body is trying to get a message to you—so stop long enough to listen and make a plan to take care of what it tells you to care for.

2. Be aware of random thoughts and flashes

Have you ever been thinking about one thing and all of the sudden, without reason, you start thinking about someone you care about or something you need to get done? I have learned to take that as a sign that my intuition is trying to shine through. I used to ignore it as intrusive, especially if I was trying to get a book written about shame-proofing your parenting! But I have gotten good at taking a few seconds to check in with those fleeting thoughts and flashes, to see what it may be about. And again, it's not a woo-woo thing; it's something that everyone experiences. So, become aware of when it happens and what you want to do to check in with it. You can stop and jot it down on your phone (almost every device has some sort of notes app). You can stop and try to link it to what's going on in your life (like if you have a flash about your child's homework and know that she tends to leave it at home). Or you can just get good at noticing that it happens (even if you're not ready to do anything with it yet). I want to caution you not to stew on these thoughts and flashes or get yourself all in a tizzy about them. Intuitive hunches appear to support and guide, not to scare or antagonize. So, if it's an agonizing thought or flash, go ahead and move on with your day without stopping to give attention to it just yet. This does not mean ignore intuition that makes you feel uncomfortable. For example, if you get a hunch that you need to apologize to your child about how you yelled the night before, listen to it. It might be uncomfortable to follow through on this hunch, but it's something that can help you build a deeper connection with your child.

3. Acknowledge that meditation is not only for yogis

Meditation is not reserved for ultra-flexible yoga teachers and super Zen Monks. It's more about learning to be still and quiet so that you can truly hear your mind. The best way to start meditating is to do it when it feels right and use guided meditation. Using meditation will help you get back to your calmness when your thoughts start to sway and help you get used to the stillness. Starting with just stillness can feel weird and cause your mind to wander quickly. For this intuition tool, start small—1-5 minutes a day—and gradually increase to a place where being still doesn't feel like the most awkward thing ever. I suggest guided meditations, because the voice on meditation tracks can help soothe you into calmness until you learn to slow your mind down enough to just listen to white noise. Learning to bring meditation into your life not only helps you to increase your attunement to your intuition, but it also helps you find quietness to sleep when you're normally worrying at night, and can even help you to get a better night's sleep. The idea here is not to make meditation all about being Zen, but rather use it the same way you use food: to refuel yourself emotionally and mentally.

So, what does learning to trust your intuition have to do with your parenting? Its main role is to allow you to stop looking everywhere else to find your confidence as a parent. You cannot shame-proof your parenting if you're trying all the parenting gimmicks and listening to everyone else but yourself.

Second, trusting your intuition helps you connect with your child. Punishment often creates barriers, not just with your child but in every other aspect of your life as well. When we are reprimanded in a way that feels impersonal, we begin to believe that the person laying down the law doesn't truly understand us or our motives, and this creates a disconnect that can only be repaired by removing the punishment and getting to know the person. When you ignore your intuition about your child and move straight to what you think others want you to do, you create a disconnect. After years of this disconnect, it can be difficult to meet your child's needs and be their guide, because they assume that they'll be punished instead of understood. And getting back to your intuition helps lay the foundation for understanding, which leads to connections, which in turn supports finding solutions for your child's behavior.

What do you think your kid needs?

As I mentioned earlier when discussing intuition and trusting your gut, many parents know exactly what their child needs, but are often led astray based on what they think others want them to do.

But now that you're equipped with tools to begin to trust your intuition a bit more, let's revisit the idea of knowing what your child needs.

Before we begin exploring this reflective tool and how it will support you in shame-proofing your parenting, we need to distinguish between needs, wants, desires, and expectations.

Needs

Needs are the things we must have in order to survive in life. Oxygen, water, food, sleep: these are all needs. But along with these biological needs, there are also emotional and mental needs that we all have. When you look at Maslow's Hierarchy of Needs[5] (refer to diagram) you can see that after we've managed to supply our physiological needs, we have the safety needs (finances, shelter, well-being), the need to belong (friendships, intimate partnerships), the need for esteem (feeling respected), and the need for self-actualization (living to one's full potential).

Wants

Wants are defined as things that we think we need but actually don't. We often feel the same intense emotion for getting what we want as we do when we are denied what we need. In the grand scheme of things, the cultures that we live in teach us more about what we should have, which often blurs the lines of what we need and what we want. A great rule of thumb to use to assess a want is to ask yourself: Will I die if I don't have this?

Desires

Desires, in this sense, are a bit more evasive than wants, because they include not only what society says we should covet, but also include our fantasies and imaginative creativity. Desires can come from unrealistic expectations (i.e., we desire to look like the model on a magazine cover), fantasies about outcomes (i.e., we desire to win the lottery by playing our lucky numbers), and/or things we've created from our imagination (i.e., we desire having the ability to fly so we can get through traffic more easily). Desires are often ignored and dismissed when we are in a supportive state. But when mixed with shame and guilt, desire can become the framework for how we see ourselves and our children.

---

5   Maslow, A. (2013). A theory of human motivation. College Station, TX, United States: Rough Draft Printing.

Expectations

Expectations are the things we feel need to happen to reach a specific goal. When we set tasks or goals for our children, we expect that the way we raised them, the limits we've set, their age/maturity, and the values we taught them will all work together to help our children get the task accomplished. But one aspect of expectations that we often ignore is that they often come from our wants and desires without any real understanding of the person's abilities to actually complete the task.

But one aspect of expectations that we often ignore is that they often come from our wants and desires without any real understanding of the person's abilities to actually complete the task.

(See the following page for how Maslow's Hierarchy of Needs operates in the shame-proof parenting framework.)

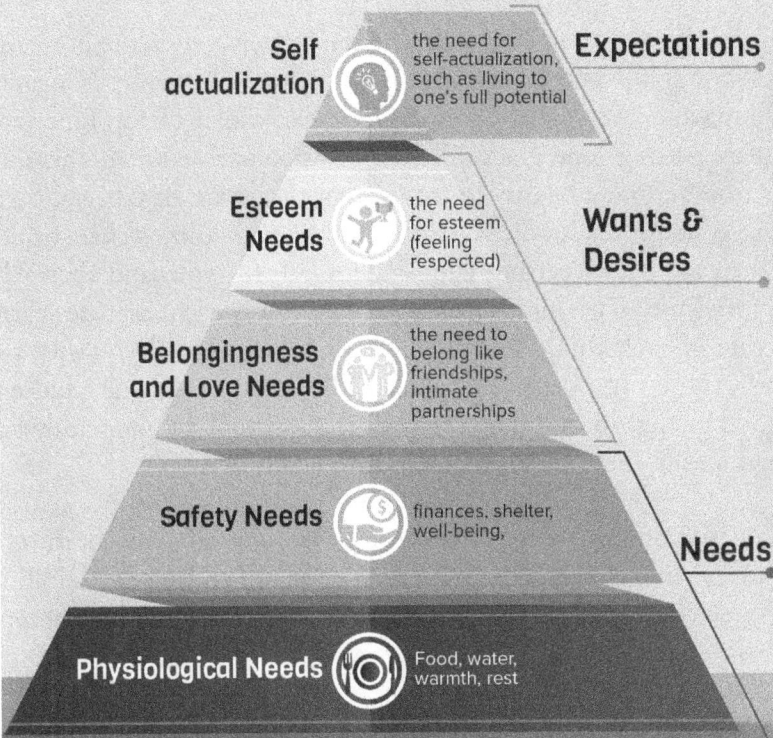

Maslow's Hierarchy of Needs in The Shame Proof Parenting Paradigm

Self actualization — the need for self-actualization, such as living to one's full potential — Expectations

Esteem Needs — the need for esteem (feeling respected) — Wants & Desires

Belongingness and Love Needs — the need to belong like friendships, intimate partnerships

Safety Needs — finances, shelter, well-being, — Needs

Physiological Needs — Food, water, warmth, rest

Reference: Adapted from Maslow, A. H. (1943). A Theory of Human Motivation. Psychological Review, 50(4), 370-96.

© Copyright 2017 Mercedes Samudio, LCSW

With those concepts in mind, let me direct you back to the question: What do you think your child needs?

As you begin to think about the answer to that question, I'll challenge you to think about the above distinctions between wants, needs, desires, and expectations.

Being able to distinguish between the four is where our true humanness shines through, whether we want it to or not. For example, which of the four would you label chores? Or under which of the four would you place getting good grades? When we ask ourselves where these ideas come from, it might be easy to answer that chores are an expectation and getting good grades is a need. But look back at Maslow's chart of needs and then ask where getting good grades falls for you, and then where does it fall for your child. Of course, we want our children to learn to take care of their things and their home, which is why you give them chores. And it's not the most far-fetched idea to expect our children to get good grades, so that they can pass grade school and hopefully go to college, and so they can start a financially stable career.

Still, questioning where these ideas came from and how they fit into your parenting, will give you more space for empathy and more flexibility to have open discussions about these common convictions we have accepted as needs.

When you can get good at distinguishing among these concepts for your child, you can be more of a guide for them as opposed to bee-lining straight for punishment. Understanding that a need is something we must have to feel fulfilled as humans, whereas wants, desires, and expectations are all up for debate, can actually give you more space to shed your perfectionist cover that seemingly comes with being a parent. And you can be more of a model for authentic humanness for your child. You teach them that until basic needs are met, no one can solve any problems that come up for them. This is a good rule to live by for yourself: when your basic needs aren't met, it's going to be a lot harder to hold a space for your child and be a model for them.

Let's dig just a bit deeper into this complex ball of fun that is distinguishing between these four concepts. A side effect of taking the time to help your child understand the differences between these concepts, is that you get better at managing those ideas for yourself. This in turn gives you more empathy for your child. A common issue for many of the parents I work with is not knowing what they need, want, desire, or even expect of themselves. I'll ask a parent, what do you need to feel rested, or what's one desire you have for your career outside of parenting, or if you could have anything, what would you want? Out of all the variations of these questions, do you want to know what most of these parents answer? Something that has to do with their role as a parent. You might say, "Duh!" But here's why that's an issue: the more you entangle your needs, wants, desires, and expectations to your identity as a parent, the less likely you'll be able to let your child detach these concepts from you. When we get to parenting defense mechanisms, you'll learn that this way of thinking is how parents develop martyrdom. Thinking that your child should want, need, desire, and expect the same things as you—or even worse, understand why you have these ideas—can cause you to fall on the sword of parenting, killing any semblance of your whole human identity.

In these instances, I ask my parents to take a break from their parenting role during our sixty-minute session together and get to a place where the other aspects of their identity have as much value as their parenting role. When I give parents permission to do this, you can only imagine the amount of passion and drive that comes from their answers. They want to travel, they desire to finish a degree, they expect their children to make mistakes just as they do.

Witnessing this transformation in parents, simply by giving them permission to take off their parenting identity for sixty minutes, illustrates for me the bigger issue we have with not allowing parents to be wholly human when they take on the role of raising humans. Confining parents to a set of norms doesn't allow them to tap into every aspect of who they are, honoring all their life experiences, in a way that actually keeps them from having the empathy and space to do this for their children.

When we put humans in a box and tell them that they can only identify with their parenting role, this disconnects them from the other parts of themselves that make them human. We do this, then we ask these same humans to understand, give space to, and empathize with their child who has yet to be boxed in by roles and social identities. Does any of this seem right to you? How can I have empathy for an aspect of myself you have shamed me into disconnecting from?

With this explanation of learning to distinguish between needs, wants, desires, and expectations, you're on the positive path to being able to shame-proof your parenting.

> *It's not about you when they're doing great. It's not about you when they're "behaving". It's not about you when they are a mess. Best to focus on keeping yourself filled-up and regulated so you can weather the developmental storms.*
>
> *—Sarah MacLaughlin, LSW*

I took a detour into this discussion because what I want you to do is to get past the surface of your parenting and your child's behavior, and move towards a closer understanding that being human is a journey for everyone. These foundational understandings will make it possible for you to shame-proof your parenting, and seeing how shame affects the business of being human in real ways, will open up space for empathy (for both you and your child).

So, let me ask you again. *Why are you worried about giving your kid what she needs?*

Yeah, I know. I just spent a nice amount of time telling you to trust your gut and leading you to understand the difference between needs and wants. But here's the deal: I know that all that just touches the surface of why shame creeps its way into your parenting without you even noticing.

I'll share my theory: the reason why you still worry, fret, get anxious, and ignore your intuition about what your child needs is because once a specific piece of our identity gets judged, we internalize the shame it produces, and instinctively build a wall around it to protect that piece of our identity from further harm.

For example, I did a lot of my early work with families in a non-profit agency, where my role as a therapist was to support parents and children in the school system. I remember sitting in IEP meetings with parents, watching them sink lower and lower into their seats as the school personnel read page after page of psychological testing results and behavior reports about their child. By the end of many of these meetings, the parent had heard so much negative stuff about their child—mixed with sporadic instances of "But he's a good boy—he just needs some help", that they had no other recourse but to defend their parenting. It wasn't that this parent didn't want the help, but how can you hear that much negativity by a group of people you view as professionals and not feel ashamed, guilty, and small as a person? On one hand, the school personnel are attempting to do their job of educating your child and detailing the many barriers they've found to doing that job. But on the other hand, having their child, metaphorically their heart, relegated to a set of test results and behaviors, has a very negative effect on a parent. It was in those meetings, and others with helping professionals, that I began to see why parents are so defensive and sometimes combative when it comes to their child.

This example, and my theory on why you still worry, makes it difficult to take my suggestions, like developing your intuition and distinguishing between wants and needs. I get that you've developed a protective sheath over your parenting identity for fear that who you are will be attacked. But this is why shame-proofing is so integral. It gives you and your family the space to reflect, and not disconnect from one another in order to maintain your sanity. But shame-proofing is not another excuse to get defensive.

The result of constantly having to protect your parenting identity, and even the integrity of your child's reputation, is how parents develop what I call "parenting defense mechanisms." Parenting defense mechanisms are strategies parents use to keep themselves from being emotionally harmed by judgments and shaming. Those knee-jerk reactions you have to your kids' behavior? Maybe yelling or icy silence or crying? Those are your parenting defense mechanisms, which you've developed to handle your own shame. I have yet to meet a parent who doesn't have at least two parenting defense mechanisms working at any given time, and it's a direct result of the parent shaming culture we've created in this world. We will dive deeper into the phenomena of parenting defense mechanisms later on in the book.

You've never needed parenting gimmicks

If shame keeps your intuition and gut feelings hidden from your parenting identity, we know that using parenting gimmicks to manage your child's behavior does a few things:

- Decreases the stress unwanted behaviors can have on the family and on your emotional health

- Avoids the weight of feeling like a bad parent on the misfire of a parenting strategy

- Allows you to hope that it's not you and the solution is fixable without doing any deeper work

But, if you *only* use the parenting gimmick and don't do that deeper work, you'll remain in a perpetual cycle of feeling like a failure. It's hard to develop the confidence a mastery of a skill affords when you never quite grasp the real reasons you have the issue in the first place.

What I see time and time again in a parent's quest to find the right strategy, is a focus on the surface behaviors their child displays and a complete dismissal of the emotional, mental, and systemic issues at work underneath. No matter the parenting gimmick, if you never attack what's underneath the surface, it will keep bubbling back up wearing a different face. This is not a judgment on you as a parent—I just spent a nice portion of this chapter validating why it's easier to focus on those surface issues rather than going deeper. So, trust me that by reading this book, you'll get the support you need. In shame-proofing your parenting, you'll have the tools to actually tackle that deep stuff and not hide from it.

Many of the most popular parenting gimmicks shift between controlling behavior or not controlling behavior. But the real strategy lies in developing a relationship with your child, getting to know who you are and who they are, and then using that knowledge to set healthy limits that allow both you and your child to make mistakes, learn from the mistakes, and grow from the mistakes. Limit setting is not about control or restriction. It's about creating a safe environment to practice new skills and to develop a mastery of those skills so they become ingrained into your consciousness, and you can quickly access them when you're in a triggering situation. In the nonviolent child-raising paradigm that I'm certified in and teach with my private clients, the perspective is that setting limits becomes a way to support a child's development of healthy habits, as opposed to teaching the child about the harsh lessons of life.

Want to know why the parenting strategies you've tried don't work? They fail to take into account how you and your child process emotions, as well as how you and your child perceive situations. The sad truth is that no book, strategy, class, course, or expert can predict how you will use their tools, in what circumstance you will get to use them, and what state you and your child are in when you're challenged to use them.

This variability in being human can only be addressed by you and your child, in the moment and afterwards when you reflect on the moment.

But here's the sunshine: parenting gimmicks *can* work when you learn to incorporate them into your unique family system, not just use them at face value. Taking the strategy and practicing with your child through communication, reflection, and role play allow these strategies to mold and shift into your family's unique existence, so it looks more like you and your child, as opposed to Dr. Parenting Expert.

May your choices reflect your hopes, not your fears.

—Nelson Mandela

The best way to start using this deeper work method of parenting is to start learning how to fail forward. Perfectionism, shame, unrealistic expectations, past traumas, your relationship with the co-parent, and all other external forces have a small place in this way of thinking. When we learn to fail forward, we expect to fail and allow that failure to teach us what to do next.

This posture of expecting to fail but knowing that we'll learn from the failure, is so different than what many parents have inadvertently learned, which is how to fail backwards. For most parents—and maybe you've experienced this too—each time they fail at effectively using a parenting gimmick, they fall back into the familiar set of behaviors and battles, even if they know they're the cause of their current struggles.

We do this because the familiar habits are embedded in our consciousness of who we think we are as parents. The goal of failing forward helps you to shift that consciousness to failure not being a part of your identity, but rather a way to further develop your identity as a parent. Do you see the difference?

Clinging to parenting gimmicks helps to confirm the fail backward notion that we are inherently failures, which leads to a lack of empathy for ourselves and thus our children when they fail. But when we rely on failing, learning, and growing through each trial and error we encounter with our children, we can detach failure from our identity and see it more flexibly. And your children will be less afraid of failure, too.

This is essentially why I share that learning to love your own parenting style is the better decision. Despite a whole chapter on sidestepping the parenting gimmicks thrown at you, I am not averse to parenting strategies and their use. But I advocate more for your own development as a parent, as opposed to taking on the identity of whatever parenting expert or parenting fad is popular. In the end, this advice is the same as you give to your child when they want to wear a certain fashion, listen to a certain style of music, or fall into the wrong crowd. You tell them that it's a fad that will pass and that they can't jump through hoops each time the tide shifts. But, in retrospect, this is what you do when you allow the current parenting trends to validate (or invalidate) your parenting identity, so much so that you internalize the shame it brings and allow it to deter you from your intuition and your relationship with your child.

Conclusion

We've covered a lot of ground in this chapter. And I know that I have taken you on a roundabout tour of the complex nature of being a human. But, in the end, you are Dr. Parenting Expert. This walk through the forest of intuition, wants versus needs, and critique on the parenting strategies that you cling to, calls to your attention the very fine line you walk as a parent: one where you straddle between your messy humanness and the illusion that your parenting identity is untouched by this messiness. Each parenting strategy that you come across was hard won by the expert that is sharing it with you. It might do you a bit of good to perceive their strategies and ideals as an anecdote about their parenting journey, as opposed to a tried-and-true set of steps to succeed at your own parenting. Taking this theme and expanding it further into how to create your own parenting manual is another step on the path to shame-proofing your parenting.

CHOOSE YOUR OWN ADVENTURE

(AKA The Elusive Parenting Manual)

When I was 5 years old, my mother always told me that happiness was the key to life. When I went to school, they asked me what I wanted to be when I grew up. I wrote down, "happy". They told me that I didn't understand the assignment, and I told them they didn't understand life.

—John Lennon

We really suck at helping people become the stewards of a new generation! I don't mean that as a judgment, but rather as an observation. In the past chapters, we talked about how shame is created and how it affects the ways parents connect to their own identity and to their children. And it's in that discussion that I have come to the conclusion, that we are not great at helping humans develop a healthy parenting identity.

Allowing someone the time to be a great entrepreneur or a loving spouse is a concept that you would agree with me is commonplace in our society. But what's funny about this is that very few of us give a parent that time and space. Which is a shame, because a parent only really has nine months to get it together before a human is thrust upon them—and that's if you're a biological parent. If you've come into your parenting role in other ways, like adoption or kinship care, then you have an even shorter time to transition into a role that comes with no instructions or manuals. When we look at it like this, you can imagine why it's so difficult for parents to find their footing, contend with the transition of becoming a caregiver for another human, and then do it well enough, and consistently enough, for others not to shame them. This just doesn't make sense to me.

Still, as you read this book, you're likely hoping to find a set of strategies to raise healthy children. You know that a definitive parenting manual is about as imaginary as finding a secret world in the back of a wardrobe cabinet. But as you manage your own expectations and visions of your family with those of how society expects you to be, you're feeling like a manual would give you a leg up on this parenting marathon.

Well, guess what? You have the manual already! The only issue is that this manual is a living, breathing, ever changing document. Each chapter is filled with trials, errors, ups, downs, and it's infused with the uniqueness that is you and your family. This means that, unfortunately or fortunately, depending on how you see the world, you get to be the author of that elusive parenting manual. Thankfully, we'll explore the overarching concepts that you might need to include in that manual. But, remember, this is not meant to be a holy bible that you listen to without fault. As I shared, this breathing document requires reflection, communication, empathy, grace, patience, and a commitment to being authentically you, while allowing your child to do the same. This will create your unique shame-proof parenting manual: a parenting manual created from the soul and fabric of your unique family that revives your confidence, leaves space for you to develop your parenting identity, and opens you up for more connection with your child.

Breaking the differences in parenting

As we begin to jump into the general themes of your parenting manual, let me veer into the two styles of parenting you'll most likely pull from—*Old Style Parenting* and *New Style Parenting*. These two camps of parenting are what most parents in today's world are grappling with. Since you live in a generation where research and the culture of parenting has become mainstream, you have a lot of information at your fingertips. But you also ponder the benefits of how previous generations raised children without all of that and still managed to get you and other adults in your cohort out into the world as best as they could. While there is most definitely room to critique the harsher undertones of past parenting techniques, I can't ignore the fact that even the newer strategies fail to produce the behaviors we want. In that respect, I think a discussion on how these two parenting styles operate in our common consciousness is necessary, if only to give space to reflect on them so you can get closer to finding the details you need for your own unique parenting manual. As I stated earlier, simply condemning our predecessors for their parenting skills is not enough to create change in your own parenting. There must be reflection on where these ideals came from and what purpose they served. In having this understanding, you can then understand their motivations and create a new perspective on obtaining that same purpose or goal in your own unique way.

In what I call *Old Style Parenting*, our parents controlled us out of fear and love. For them, we were the most precious things in their lives and their responsibility was to get us to adulthood as healthy and useful as we could be. The harsh punishments and strict discipline was justified based on that logic. For many parents of *Old Style Parenting*, making sure that their child was safe and taken care of outweighed the long-term effects of those punishments.

Why wasn't *Old Style Parenting* as wrong as we'd like to make it out to be? In my opinion, there was no ill intention behind it; our parents honestly believed that control was the best way to raise children. Back then, not everything was child abuse.

One example that I also share from my childhood of *Old Style Parenting*, was an incident when my cousins and I were playing a game we made up called "Escape from the Island" (which entailed us jumping from one twin bed in my room to the other, trying to keep from falling in the sea, which was the floor space between the two beds). Of course, this genius idea of jumping from bed to bed, crafted by eight and nine-year-olds made sense to us, but came with some pretty unthinkable consequences: the bed broke with the weight of our successive jumping. The loud crash alerted my mother (my step-grandmother) and she raced to my room to see what the commotion was. Well, I can cut this story short and let you know that we got spankings, not only for playing in the house, but also for breaking twin beds that would cost money to get fixed. In that example, would you say that I was abused? Would you say that my mom was maliciously trying to stomp out my spirit and endanger my future emotional self? From my perspective, no, she was not. But, when we look back on *Old Style Parenting* like this we tend to demonize parents' methods for instilling values and raising children. All I'm stating is that not everything a parent did in *Old Style Parenting* was about abuse. (*Before you bash me for ignoring child abuse or romanticizing this style of parenting, keep reading.*)

In what I will call *New Style Parenting*, we were introduced to child development and the knowledge of long term effects that child-rearing had on children. We have learned that cognitive development, emotional development, and physical development are all integral aspects of what makes a human whole, and that these developmental stages begin at birth, with the majority of our development happening in childhood. We've also learned through years of research that children who are strictly controlled, often with punishments, in their youth grow up with deep scars that impede their growth in adulthood. In these studies, it was shown that emotional intelligence is just as important as moral development and intellectual development. The role of parents who use *New Style Parenting* is very like that of parents who used *Old Style Parenting*, but the burden of possibly ruining your child as a result of your parenting is felt much more with *New Style Parenting* than it was with *Old Style Parenting*. For me, the most notable research that has emerged to show us about the effects of child-rearing on humans in the long term, has been the Adverse Childhood Experiences (ACEs) study,[6] which demonstrated with accuracy and detail that negative experiences in childhood have

---

6   Adverse Childhood Experiences (ACEs), 2016. CDC.gov. Retrieved 7 December 2016, from https://www.cdc.gov/violenceprevention/acestudy/

significant effects on our emotional well-being and physical health in adulthood. One of the main thought leaders on these findings, Bessel van der Kolk, wrote a book called *The Body Keeps the Score*, that details how important it is not only to acknowledge how adverse childhood experiences affect humans as they mature, but how integral healing is in rewiring our brains to overcome these experiences.[7]

Why isn't *New Style Parenting* the Holy Grail we'd like it to be? Think back to the previous paragraph where I shared that the pressure to raise a human has been increased since we've had all this research and knowledge thrown at us. Not only has this created a generation of parents who are more anxious and worried about their parenting, but it has also created a culture of parent shaming that gives every person with a voice permission to blame parents for all the ills of the world. While we condemn parents who use *Old Style Parenting* and label them child abusers, we also condemn parents who use *New Style Parenting* for refusing to set strong limits on their child.

> *"Parenting behaviour is a direct reflection of the quality and quantity of support available for the parent throughout their lives. All humans contain the potential for profound love and devotion, subject to their own state of emotional nourishment."*
>
> *—Robin Grille, Parenting For A Peaceful World*

As I said earlier, I don't want to romanticize either parenting style, nor ignore that child abuse unfortunately occurs under both paradigms. For instance, in *Old Style Parenting*, abuse came in the form of corporal punishment used with the intent of keeping your child in line. While in *New Style Parenting*, emotional abuse became more prevalent out of

---

7   Van der Kolk, B. The body keeps the score: Brain, mind, and body in the healing of trauma. 1st ed. New York: Penguin Books, 2014

a parents' desperate need to control their child without hitting, and a fear of getting a CPS report. Essentially, I am in the camp of voices that believes we can no longer be okay with the harsh punishments of the past, but we also cannot condemn our parents for not having the new knowledge while raising us. What I do want to do, however, is get you thinking about how you view parenting, and how you don't have to have tunnel vision when it comes to raising your child. Being open and adaptable forms the basis for creating your own shame-proof parenting manual, and it encompasses the idea that when you know better, you do better!

Some of the bigger questions in reflecting on your parenting views, to get you thinking about how you will create your own parenting manual, include:

- How do we bring back the idea of setting the boundaries our parents set for us, but still be able to provide a nurturing space that allows our children to grow into healthy adults?

- How do we bridge the gap of past discipline with present research?

- And how do we raise parents who feel confident setting limits and giving love without having to pick one over the other in managing their child's unwanted behaviors?

Well if you want my answer, it's this: we stop the elitism that comes with education and knowledge, and we start realizing that none of the knowledge and research can penetrate our parenting consciousness without first realizing that we're all fallible humans. No amount of over or under parenting can make a human perfect, and no style of parenting can iron out the wrinkles of being a living, breathing human.

And that uncertainty is what scares us. In our haste to create perfection, we've created chaos; we've created factions of parenting that pits strict discipline against nurturing child-raising; we've made monsters out of ignorance and gods out of education. While there are people who hurt their children regardless of what they do or do not know (this is where a discussion on child abuse can be had), there are many more parents straddling the fence of being a monster or a god. The bloody fight between these two sides shows up in our cultural need to shame, and the internal guilt we each feel if we choose one over the other.

Taking the steps to create your parenting manual

That detour into how we've pieced together our parenting consciousness (both on an individual and societal level), along with the discussion in the last chapter on learning to rely on your own intuition as a parent, helps to lay the foundation for developing your shame-proof parenting identity. Now, we'll look at one of the other aspects of your parenting identity. This aspect relies on the skills of critical thinking and analytical reasoning, skills that are just as important for you now, as they were throughout your education.

The critical thinking I want to explore, as it relates to parenting, is a bit different than what you learned in school, though. Academically, critical thinking means that you use clear, rational analysis that includes critique to find the answer/solution.[8] While I could just rely on that definition for parenting, the definition that I have created for parental critical thinking is this:

> *Use of rational and empathetic reasoning to analyze strategies and tools that will support and guide you and your child to finding solutions.*

---

8   Walters, K. Re-thinking reason: New perspectives in critical thinking (1st ed.). Albany (NY): State University of New York Press, 1994.

Much as teenagers learn how to think critically through a fiction book that's full of conflicts and unexpected plot twists, parents can use their own critical thinking when navigating their child's conflicts and behavior.

With the idea of parental critical thinking established, I guess the next most salient encouragement I can give you as we talk about creating your own parenting manual is this: choose your own adventure as you journey with your child, and make and accept the decisions that can either hinder or bolster your child's human development.

We're not raising kids that need managing; we are raising humans that need to learn how to navigate life's adventures: wholly, healthily, efficiently!

When a child is born, they will not become human; they already *are* human. Your child is currently a developing human, who will eventually need less involvement from you and who will need to take care of herself, be a fulfilled person, and live a thriving life as an adult. The differences in life stages—infant, toddler, child, tween, teen, young adult, adult—are phases of human development. The phase that your child is in does not take away the fact that she's already a human. You and your children are always human, all the time.

Throughout the remainder of this chapter, I will be walking you through creating your very own parenting manual, which will be a living, breathing document. Let's start with a simple question: *What tools did you have for navigating your own life when you became a legal adult at age eighteen?*[9]

---

9   Author Note: Although the research suggests that most humans are considered fully developed by 25 years old, the American culture still sees children as adults at 18, both socially and legally, so all other things being equal, let's just say that you and your child are using the same metric. Your family will look different, but for the sake of argument, we're saying that 18 years is when your child may be ready to launch into their adult life stage.

Think about the following areas of life all humans attempt to master:

- *Peer relationships*

- *Intimate relationships*

- *Professional Development*

- *Academic/Intellectual pursuits*

- *Life goals and ambitions*

- *Family relationships*

- *Health: physical, emotional, mental*

- *Environment: home life, recreation, work*

- *Spiritual Development*

As you reflect on the question above, reflect on this question as well:

What tools/strategies do you want your children to have when they turn 18?

These questions have no right or wrong answers. They are not baiting questions to see if you're doing the parenting thing "right." But these two questions challenge you to think about and reflect upon what you were given to move into your adult phase, AND what you'd like to give your child as they make that transition.

One thing I know, no parent has ever told me they want their child to leave their care with tons of guilt, shame, and emotional baggage. But that's exactly what you may have left your family of origin with. And if not, then I think it's at least safe to say that you left your childhood phase and moved into your adult phase with some tools missing.

The good news is that by just taking time to reflect on these questions, you have already changed the course of what your child will launch into life with. But the bad news is that no matter how much you reflect, buy into parenting strategies, gain knowledge on human behavior, and even do your own healing work, you cannot shield your child from moving into their adult stage without some form of baggage, and without all the tools they need to live thriving lives.

Our greatest glory is not in never falling but in rising every time we fall.

—Confucius

Remember when I led you on a discussion about human behavior? In that discussion, we talked about shame stories and how important it is to not stop your child from experiencing pain, but how important it is that you support and guide them through that pain.

Even as you struggle to be a better parent than yours were (or try to bring their positive energy to your parenting), you still have a separate human in your care who will experience life very differently than you did. He will have joys and successes, but he will also experience failures and pain. She will hear what you say, and she will ignore what you say. He will make the right decisions, and he will inevitably fall for the wrong advice. But here's the silver lining in all that: It's not because of you or your parenting; it's literally all a part of human behavior. While there is a lot you can shield yourself and your child from, there is even more that you'll have to guide and ride through with them.

Strategy and your parenting manual

This isn't a truth that I want you to hold onto and perceive as a "throw your hands up, your family is doomed" scenario. Rather, I want you to allow this truth to shift your perspective from assuming you know the outcomes of every decision your child will make. Letting go of the idea that you must control them to make sure they don't fail, allows you to lean into the human journey of choosing your own adventure and being able to use parental critical thinking to be a guide for your child.

I'd like to posit this theory: we fall back on strategies because of shame. We have been led to believe that as parents we can bypass our human mistakes by using the strategies of those who obviously know more than we do. Our life experiences, our past narratives, our current functioning, and our detachment from our infallible humanness have led us to trust others' instincts and strategies and ignore our own. Strategies only work when they become a part of how we see and perceive the world. No matter the expert, the research, or the popularity, a strategy will not meet our ultimate goals, because we have yet to do the work to align our perspective to match the step-by-step process we are given.

Want proof?

Look around at how many email programs you've signed up for, how many months of unused membership your gym has taken from you, how many meals you've had to throw away because they went bad while you struggled with changing your diet, and the list goes on. The strategy is always a means to an end; it is never the real issue, nor is it the way to create real change.

When parents bring me on board as a parenting coach, they usually think they need an expert to tell them how to be a good parent OR how to manage their child's behavior. But as we venture into our sessions, the parent and I begin to realize that the ways in which the family perceives each other's roles and what it means to execute and live in those roles are the main barriers. We figure out that the strategies the parent and family need are predicated on how the family wants to shift that perspective, and how much the family is ready to let go of the roles that have caused so much conflict in the family. And that process is a bit deeper and takes a bit longer than just getting some strategies.

Let me remind you, having a plan or strategy is better than nothing, as I've stated already. But after years of working with parents to support them as they create change in their families, I have no doubt that the strategies you greatly need are unique to you and your parenting; they aren't going to be found in generic parenting courses or books.

What strategies do accomplish, however, is to show you that change does need to occur. If you're reaching out for support through parenting strategies, your level of awareness is at the right stage to start the change process. And, for that, strategies are beneficial.

But what I encourage is that once the strategies fail to produce the changes you wish to see, don't give up. Be assertive in creating a parenting manual that is unique to you, your parenting style, your child(ren)'s humanness, and your family's unique barriers.

When creating your parenting manual, rather than finding one set of parenting strategies to hold onto for dear life, be open to combining an eclectic mix of what's out there to create a style for each child. That way, your relationship with them will support them in transitioning into their adult stage with a good set of tools that will help them start off life well, and leave room for them to acquire more healthy tools as they mature.

To guide you in compiling your unique parenting manual, here are some areas you may want to include:

Strategies that encourage identity development

The strategies that you find to help you encourage your child's identity development need to be based in communication and connection. As I have worked with families, I have learned that since we are social creatures, we develop our identities based on those we interact with. If you and your child begin to disconnect, bring connection back to that relationship by simply communicating and being honest about feelings.

Oftentimes, I see parents shift away from this because they don't want to hear their child's struggles, or they want to fix their child's struggles. But a child's identity doesn't develop from tough love, nor from fixing all their problems for them. Rather, as humans, we develop our identities and feel comfortable in our roles when we have the space to exist fully, and are accepted for our flaws unconditionally. It's hard to accept someone when you don't communicate with them, and it's even harder to communicate when you're not given the space to be authentic—flaws and all. One strategy that you might want to add to this section of your parenting manual is having a date with your child. This allows you to do things together that are outside of your daily parent-child activities and gives you both space to just be.

The overarching concept for adding strategies to this section is that you want to give space for the spectrum of experiences that your child will have, resist the urge to predict the future of their decisions with assumptions, and get comfortable in the mess of their experience. This means that you have to get comfortable in your own mess as well; not wallow in your flaws, but rather get comfortable knowing that for every hard-won piece of wisdom you have to give, you've most likely received it from making mistakes. It's in this awareness that you can find strategies that will help you guide your child's development towards a healthy identity.

Strategies that support the development of emotional intelligence

As you search for strategies that help build your child's emotional development, think about where you are in your journey of emotional development. Some of us are more emotional than others and we don't all express our emotions the same way. In this section of your parenting manual, find strategies that validate everyone's ways of expressing emotions and celebrate that emotions are part of the human experience, as opposed to being nuisances to our daily lives. In your parenting role, it can be easy to detach from your emotions, in an attempt to help your child get through theirs. But all that does is stop you from being empathetic to what your child is experiencing. Instead, help your children develop a feelings vocabulary that gives them words to express themselves. Make sure you model how you use these feelings words, too. If you're not someone who's big on expressing their emotions, you can bet that your child will learn to either hide their emotions, or they will look for more maladaptive ways to share how they feel. I know that many of us have learned from our own journeys that emotions are bad or a burden. But your child has not had those experiences yet, nor do they know what to do with these intense emotions that they are experiencing. The next time that your child has a meltdown or tantrum, I encourage you to see it as an opportunity to teach your child how to express herself. This process will take time. Some feeling words, your child will pick up on and begin using effortlessly, while others will take longer as you both work to find out what need they are trying to express. If you're getting stuck in this section, think about your own emotional development, your own emotional intelligence, and give yourself the empathy and space to grow as well. The lack of self-empathy for their own process is usually the biggest barrier to a parent becoming a guide for their child's emotional development.

Strategies that encourage empathetic and supportive social strategies

This section is the most fun if you're committed to being a shame-proof family. I say this because the essence of being shame-proof means that you will express yourself more authentically around your children without the fear that it will change your relationship as their caregiver. When you look for strategies to add to this section, communication will be a big factor again, but so will active listening and the creation of a safe space to problem solve social situations. I see the biggest barrier to this section being the parent's own perception and assumptions around how their child is to behave socially, instead of being open to watching their child work through social situations. This can feel, and will be, one of the toughest aspects of being a guide for your child. But remember when we talked about finding strategies that represent the child you have versus the child you want? This is the section where that will apply the most. For strategies here, look for ways to learn more about how your child thinks and processes information. For example, if your child is a kinesthetic learner (where they learn and process information most effectively through touch or doing), then helping them find social settings where they can do something physical will give them the best spaces to develop healthy social skills. Finding more about how your child processes things requires you to listen, not lecture or give advice, but listen in a way that shows that you are following their logic, not infusing the statements with your own biases. This can be difficult to do, but a suggestion I often offer my parents is to always ask your child: do you want some suggestions from me or were you just sharing your ideas with me? Using this question keeps you actively listening in the conversation, but it also stops you before you jump into solving a situation for your child. Even when they ask for advice, help them walk through what feels comfortable for them (remember the identity building stuff? You'll use it here to ask them questions that will help them think about how they see the world, versus trying to do things the ways others do it), because they'll be more likely to follow through on a suggestion if it aligns with their current perception of the world.

Strategies that support brain development

In my opinion, one of the most relevant experts on brain development as it relates to parents and raising children is Dr. Daniel Siegel. I often refer to his book (co-authored by Dr. Tina Bryson), *The Whole Brain Child: 12 Revolutionary Strategies to Nurture Your Child's Developing Mind*. This book discusses how the brain develops, what is needed to develop healthy brains, and how connection is the cornerstone of this development. As you look for strategies that are unique to your parenting and your child, think about how you can help your child not only develop logically but also how you can keep them curious about learning. Too often, we let the academic culture dictate where our child's intelligence lies, which can sometimes steal away a child's natural curiosity to learn and explore. In addition to your child's academic career, I would encourage you to look for other ways to help your child display his thinking skills and ability to learn. I know that many traditional learning institutions have done away with alternative learning—like music, shop class, etc.—but I think there is enough in our world that you can engage with your child and expose them to. For example, when your child is not doing well in school, take the focus off grades for a while and dig into what you notice your child excelling in. Does she know how to take apart things in the house and put them back together? Does he have an affinity for others' emotions and giving great advice to others? These are all measures of intelligences that our school systems don't always notice, but can boost your child's confidence in their cognitive abilities and even provide a bridge for how they perceive and process the more traditional subjects.

Strategies that encourage healthy parent-child relationship building

I have one intervention that I love for this, so I will share it with you along with an example of how I've seen it play out. While this is not the only way to build your relationship with your child, it does encourage the theme of being authentically human that I have been focusing on throughout this book. Along with this intervention, I would say that strategies that encourage you both to get outside of your daily roles will help tear down barriers and bridge gaps between you and your child, in a way that helps you both connect as humans on this life journey together, as opposed to you being over them as someone who has transcended the normal human experiences (which is how children I've worked with often see their parents, when the parents stay solely focused on their parenting role and never let their guard down for their child).

Another book that does a great job at sharing great strategies for building a healthy relationship with your child is *Playful Parenting* by Lawrence J. Cohen, Ph.D. There's a chapter titled "Follow Your Child's Lead" that gives you permission to be human with your child, and it complements the shame-proof parenting discussion we're having here.

Another strategy I recommend you add to your unique parenting manual is called the "No Roles Intervention."

The basic premise is that we take away the weight of our title and role in our family. The humans in this family are not mom, dad, sister, brother, son, or daughter. They are just humans at different intervals in their human journey who have all converged at this particular place and time to support each other. No one has all the power; issues are resolved based on who has the most effective solution, and disagreements are settled by respecting each other's viewpoints before coming to a conclusion. This may sound *Pleasantville* to you. And the first few times I did this with parents, they all laughed at the notion of giving their children equal footing in a discussion without threat of their parent's power. However, it was in these seemingly *Pleasantville* sessions that each member of the family was able to see each other clearly. It's very easy to hide behind the power, expectations, societal norms, and myths of our identities. Kids often feign ignorance because they know they can in this life stage. Parents often feign knowledge because they know they can intimidate their child into believing what they want. On a more positive note, parents sometimes hide behind their parenting role so they don't have to show their vulnerability, while kids often allow their parents to think that they aren't experiencing the spectrum of emotions all humans feel, for fear that they will upset their parents. It's in these moments of hiding that we have the most conflict. If the parent is operating from a stance of power, hiding vulnerability and feigning knowledge—and the kid is feigning ignorance and refusing to show their acknowledgement of their fluctuating emotions—it's no wonder families have conflict. You can't solve a conflict when all the parties involved are hiding. You can't get to the bottom of an issue when all those involved aren't revealing every complex experience they've had that has lead them to have the perspective they are presenting.

Thus, the "No Roles" intervention, when done with someone who understands how to undo and redo the roles in the family without damaging the family, can be an amazing experience of healing and growth.

One family I did this with included a mom, dad, teen brother, and school-age sister. The conflicts in this family were the same as many families: sibling discord, inconsistency in setting limits, parenting style differences, and overall stress from roles each member had outside the family (school, work, youth sports). As I worked with the family to get better at listening to one another before trying to resolve issues, I found that even family meetings were falling into all out blame fests, where everyone was pointing the finger at someone else because no one wanted to be named "the cause" of the issues in the family. No matter how many times I helped them understand that there was no single person who caused the tension in the family, this family had a difficult time not blaming things on each other. It got so bad that the mom called me crying, saying that they had to stop the family meetings because it was tearing the family further apart. Now, for me, this is a great place for a family to be in. I often use family meetings to expose the amount of disconnect that has slyly and pervasively haunted the family. It's good to know that a family is this disconnected, because it allows me to see what support they need to reconnect.

It was after that phone call, and a text from the teen that he didn't think his family would ever learn to like each other, that I offered them this intervention. I did so as an extended session (instead of 60 minutes, we did 90 minutes). While the parents were not excited about this initially, seeing the enthusiasm of their kids to try something different swayed them to agree to do it.

I started the session explaining how it would look: no one would have the safety of their title to shield their feelings, ideas, and/or behaviors. The parents agreed that nothing that was discussed would be reprimanded with punishment, and the kids agreed that they would not use their parents' vulnerability against them to get something they wanted later (or try to wiggle out of a punishment). Again, since everyone was new to this, I let them know that if I saw either person slipping into their role for safety, I would call it out and they'd have to state the idea again without their role as a safety net.

The first 30 minutes of this was fun. (Mostly everyone being complete asses to one another, saying what they always wanted to say and taking small jabs at each other.) But an interesting thing happened after everyone got that off their chests.

Humor began to seed its way into the siblings. They began quoting movies at each other as inside jokes as friends would do, and the sister even called the brother out on how he treated his girlfriends, asking him how he would like it if when she had a boyfriend he did that to her. That turned into a 15-minute conversation showing that he thought she was really strong and that no boy could get by doing that, how he felt he had to because all the guys who got girlfriends were dicks at his school, and the sister offering up the zinger that if he has to change himself to get a girl then maybe he shouldn't be dating yet. Everyone was fascinated by this conversation, because these two had never shared more than a minute together before where they were not fighting or arguing.

The next 30 minutes or so included the family—again without acknowledging the power, expectations, or safety of their roles—divulging into laughter, advice, sharing stories about what they do outside of their family, and how they each had goals and aspirations that sometimes differed from what they displayed to each other in their family. The mom shared at one point that she was to be a dancer until she damaged her ankle and just gave up because her mom (the kids' grandmother who was still alive) told her that she was too fat and that all that weight was why she'd hurt her ankle. As she told this story crying, the dad who usually didn't talk about feelings, stayed in his logical world, and very rarely shared any humor, shared that he'd always hated dancers anyway because they were too skinny. This worked in this family because humor, sarcasm, and inside jokes were what connected them.

Now, you might be thinking that this is all a very happy ending. But here's what happened for that family that hadn't been exposed until that night: they all realized that they weren't so different, and that each member had a strength and a weakness that, when acknowledged and respected, could help each member work. I worked with them for a few more sessions, and guess what? They still argued and had disagreements, but they were able to find solutions that were less likely to continue the disconnect. Meaning even though they got mad at each other, it was no longer about attacking and defending, but more about recognizing what that person was probably feeling, and helping them get better at asking for what they needed, rather than being mean to each other. For the parents, this meant not using their power to get their needs met, but taking time to understand what they wanted done and working to get it done together with their children.

It's not an easy experience to listen to one another. And I do advocate that family members try not to ignore conflict, but rather lean into it. Conflict can often be a negative word in our relationships, but when you learn how to have conflict in a healthy way, even without giving up your roles, you realize that each person is just trying to get their needs met, not trying to destroy you or your family.

I know that I offered two parenting books to add to your collection, but as I said earlier, I don't hate parenting books or want to discredit my contemporaries in this field. What I hope is that part of your own manual and your shame-proof parenting, is that you find the confidence to trust yourself as much as you trust another parenting expert. The books that I shared, I recommend to my private clients all the time, with the suggestion that they weave what they learn into their own unique brand of raising healthy humans.

While you can definitely find other areas to focus on, these are the five areas (strategies that develop identity, emotional intelligence, empathetic and supportive social strategies, brain development, and healthy parent-child relationship building) that coincide with the areas of life all humans needs healthy tools for. The parenting manual that you create (whether tangibly in an actual manual or not) will be such a great mix of who you are, who your child is, and the parenting philosophies that you feel complement your family the best.

Although we all say there is no parenting manual, you can now say that you DO have the manual for your family. It's a living document that is constantly evolving and growing with you and your family.

Conclusion

Shame-proof parenting is not about focusing solely on one style of parenting or holding to one set of parenting techniques. Rather, it's about being open to the fluidity and constant flow of raising a human while still being human yourself. As you learn to create your shame-proof parenting manual, what I empower you to focus on is building a sense of confidence that embodies the notion that, no matter how you raise your human, the best measure of how you're doing is your constant awareness that you are on a journey together. It's not you against them, or you over them. This awareness will be the foundation of your parenting manual, and it will even give you the assurance that you are on the right path. Essentially, the merging of all these instances and styles of parenting occurs when we acknowledge that our parents were doing the best they could, and so are we. What's more important, though, is that we can look at how each style of parenting gives us knowledge and research that we didn't have before, but we cannot forget to trust that we are the best person to raise the human we were given. We don't need to be anything more than exactly who we are. As we go through the sections of building your parenting manual, the fluidity can feel scary but if we commit to doing it together with our child, let's throw in a supportive and empathetic community, mix it with a society that wants to end parent shaming, and top it off with our own unique parenting powers. A recipe like this can heal the wounds of the past and bring forth a generation of parents and children who can exist as whole humans.

SHAME-PROOF YOUR PARENTING: LAYING THE GROUNDWORK

Be who you needed when you were younger.

—Unknown

The whole book has lead up to this moment! After learning about my own journey into shame and how it's led me to be where I am today, having discussions about where your parenting shame may come from, what it looks like to trust your own humanness on your parenting journey, and getting an overview of the components for creating your own parenting manual, you are now in a reflective space to dig into how to shame-proof your parenting.

The concept for shame-proofing came from the idea of wanting to end parent shaming. If you follow me on my social media profiles, you may have seen the hashtag, #EndParentShaming. I have a whole campaign around how we, as a society, can become more aware of how we're shaming parents, and the consequences that come from that culture. But like everything else that we try to change in society, it all starts with the individual. I realized that we might have a tough time ending parent shame if parents themselves aren't aware of how that shame affects them and their identity as parents.

So, I reflected: what would it look like if parents and their families could create a sort of protection around themselves to withstand the shame thrown at them?

That question drove me to look wider, not just at shame-proofing parents but also at the concept of shame-proofing families. How could families work together to achieve this and to become healthy together?

So, what is shame-proof parenting?

When you're led by shame-proof parenting, your family will understand each other enough that when people come against you, you won't buckle under the pressure and you won't turn on each other. You and your family can feel confident in saying, "This is our journey, this is where we are right now," without worrying about others' judgments.

Once you have shame-proofed your parenting, you can ask for support when you need to and not feel like you must follow certain prescriptions about what support you're supposed to want. You learn to be comfortable with the trial-and-error routine of parenting, allowing yourself to learn and grow, both as a human and a parent. You get to ask people who question, judge, or attempt to shame you if they'd rather have the chance to learn more about what you're doing with your family, or would like to just judge you based on what they think they know.

At the end of the day, shame-proofing your parenting means that you make it more difficult for external forces to penetrate your family's connection, and instead you come back in to each other and figure out how to deal with problems together.

But let me get one thing straight: Shame-proofing your parenting in no way means that you are perfect, or that your shame-proof family will always work together harmoniously.

When you stop living your life based on what others think of you, real life begins. At that moment, you will finally see the door of self-acceptance opened.

—Shannon L. Adler

The point in shame-proofing your parenting is to give you and your family a space to regroup when a conflict or drama enters your relationship.

No one can reflect and grow while they are fighting and defending themselves. No matter how resilient you are alone, your parenting is a lot more resilient when you and your family all agree that you're going to tackle life together.

But making the first steps towards shame-proof parenting is going to be a challenge, so let's look at what barriers will come up for you as you make this movement to bring more shame-proofing into your parenting.

Parenting defense mechanisms

I mentioned parenting defense mechanisms earlier in the book, but now we're going to dive into what that looks like for shame-proofing your parenting. Your parenting defense mechanisms are going to flare up as soon as you start implementing the first shame-proofing steps. The idea of parenting defense mechanisms is much like the other defenses you may know about. But instead of them being a barrier to your growth as an individual, the parenting defense mechanisms also block your relationship with your parenting identity and your relationship with your child.

If you're not familiar with the term defense mechanisms, let me give you a brief definition of how they are used in the mental health world. Defense mechanisms are "manners in which we behave or think in certain ways to better protect or 'defend' ourselves." [10] In psychology, these strategies are ranked and categorized by how they work in our lives and how primitive they are. The idea is that the more juvenile a defense mechanism, the less likely it is to sustain you over the long term. However, in the case of parenting defense mechanisms, there is no ranking. These strategies work because they fall in line with how we see parenting in our society, which further confirms that shaming and judging parents creates more harm than good, more stagnation than change.

---

10   Grohol, J. 15 common defense mechanisms, 2016. Retrieved 5 October 2016, from http://psychcentral.com/lib/15-common-defense-mechanisms/

Parenting defense mechanisms are the strategies that parents use to protect themselves and their parenting identity from shame, judgment, and the frustration that comes with raising a human while still being humans themselves.

With parenting defense mechanisms, the idea is that all the negative external experiences you have built up over time, all the times you've had to defend yourself from judgment, each time you've had to explain your parenting only to be ignored or ridiculed, and every time that you have laid awake at night wondering if this parenting thing is even worth it, you have built up barriers and walls that helped you stay sane. And for that, your parenting defense mechanisms are helpful. Where they hurt, however, is when you continue to use them instead of being reflective and growing from those experiences of being criticized. That's where shame-proofing your parenting comes in: when you can protect yourself from the external forces that influence how you see yourself as a parent, you make space to reflect on what was said, done, and experienced—and you can grow from there!

When you let your parenting defense mechanisms grow, they begin to protect you unconsciously and they create impenetrable walls that make it hard for your family to connect, and make it harder for you to acknowledge when you're doing well. These strategies begin to define who you think you are as a parent, and it distances you from seeking support when you truly need it!

All in all, parenting defense mechanisms protect you in the short term, but become barriers to healing for you and your family in the long term.

This isn't another judgment, nor is it something you should feel bad about. This is an awareness for helping you learn what's under the shame and guilt, what's under the connection (or disconnection) with your child, and what it means to develop and create a healthy parenting identity.

What are the most common parenting defense mechanisms?

Deflection

This strategy is present when you take the spotlight off yourself and highlight another aspect of your identity, and/or make a statement about the other person's identity. A common example of this strategy is: "You're not a parent yet."

We have been fed this myth that because someone else is a parent they must understand what you're going through. And while that is often true, the opposite is true as well: not all parents have the same experiences and cannot always relate to your parenting journey. We have also come to believe that people who have not been parents can't comprehend what it feels like to have the weight of parenting on their shoulders. Both perspectives help exacerbate the use of this parenting defense mechanism, so much so that it makes it difficult to hear ideas and advice that might be helpful or useful.

Parents use this one a lot. And I don't blame them. It can be hard to constantly hear what others think about your parenting identity and the strategies you use to raise your child. It can be a lot easier to shut it all out with the idea of telling someone that they don't understand, or that they don't know what it means to have this experience. But the interesting part of this is that when someone has another perspective from you, it can shed light on a piece of your experience that you haven't looked at yet. So, this parenting defense mechanism can keep you from growing and seeing your parenting identity in another way.

How to manage this defense mechanism:

Look at the person who is talking to you. Are they close to you? Do you trust their ideas? Do you believe they are providing helpful ideas, even if it's not in the best way? If you check in with your intuition and truly answered yes to those questions, but you're not ready to hear what they have to say (or you need more space to process what they've said), try saying something like: "I really appreciate your support, do you mind if I share with you what I need and maybe we can brainstorm some ways for me to meet that need?" The language here isn't as important as the concept; you want to have the support but you also want the person to truly see the work you've put in already, so they know where to go with their advice.

Isolation

Isolation can, at times, be a useful strategy, but like all the parenting defense mechanisms it can also be debilitating and lonely. I have seen so many parents stay away from friends, not return to support groups, ignore party invites and family gatherings, for fear that either their kid will display some behavior that is unacceptable or that they'll have to defend their parenting yet again. And, in this strategy, you feel that you can protect your child and your sanity by just staying away. This strategy can really backfire when you truly need support and/or you do finally decide to participate in activities. This is because isolating yourself and your child doesn't allow you to build up the resilience and confidence you need to sustain the imperfection that is in the world. Yes, people are horrible at times. No, people don't think before they speak. But at the end of the day, you get to stand up for your parenting and your family, and you don't have to be aggressive about it.

Isolation also comes from the expectations we have of ourselves and our children. If you expect your child to never act out on a public outing, and then they do, you're more likely to isolate from that type of outing in the future instead of reflecting on what occurred that instigated your child's behavior. When you isolate for this reason, you and your child never get the chance to find solutions to the issue, and instead you both internalize the feelings of frustration and failure, leading to more isolation and less support from others.

How to manage this defense mechanism:

Find your tribe and start there. Your tribe are the people you feel the most comfortable with, people who know you, who accept you, and who don't feel the need to advise you all the time. Get good at practicing what you want to say about certain issues that commonly come up for your family, with this core group of people. Stop forcing yourself to be around people who don't make you feel good (and yes, that includes some family members). Didn't go to the PTA meeting? So what? Missed a few of your child's classmates' birthday parties? And?! We spend so much time isolating ourselves from what we dread, that we forget we can be around people who make us feel great!

Feigning responsibility

When we feign responsibility, it's usually to get out of something. You say you've got a sick child whom you have to care for, because you no longer want to attend an event. We do it all the time. I know I have. And for parents, this looks like using kids to get out of things/obligations/relationships. This works so well when we need a break from the busyness of living on-the-go modern lives and must recharge from the role of being a parent. But it also gets us in a bind when we're ready to get back into the world. I'm not talking about being an introvert or genuinely not enjoying being around a lot of people. (Being introverted is a piece of your human identity that can be woven into your parenting identity by finding a tribe of people you actually enjoy being around). I'm talking about using your responsibility as a parent to get out of things because you fear judgment and more shame to be thrown your way. Common reasons I've heard for people feigning responsibility can include: fear of baby crying or kids acting up, child's going through some sort of developmental milestone that causes irritability, or must maintain your child's punishment so you don't want them to have the luxury of a babysitter. And while I have missed a few, I can tell you that no matter the excuse, when you feign responsibility as a defense mechanism, you illustrate to your support system that you don't think they can handle the parenting part of your identity. That makes it difficult to seek support when you're at your wit's end. Using this strategy, you are essentially taking away your supports' choice to be there for you. It's like the isolation strategy: you shield yourself from pain and shame and you close yourself off from support too.

How to manage this defense mechanism:

The best way to manage this parenting defense mechanism is to be honest when you can, and set realistic boundaries for yourself. What this looks like is not overcommitting and letting people know why you have to set boundaries about your time. If you have a child who is teething, let the person know. If they say come over anyway, and you trust that this person (or the others at the event) will be able to support you and your child's needs, then go. But here's where the shame-proofing kicks in: if you feel the opposite, this is not the time to be polite. You can explain that you're going to bow out of this event so that you can focus on helping your child through his teething, but that you'll do your best to attend the next one. This is different than feigning responsibility, because you're being true to yourself and your child's needs, as opposed to feeling like you have to cover up or make an excuse to spare someone else's feelings.

Projection

This one is a common defense mechanism for everyone, but it looks a bit different when used by parents. Outside of your parenting identity, projection is taking your negative emotions and throwing them at someone (or something) else who was not the cause of those emotions. As a parenting defense mechanism, projection has the added factor of guilt thrown in from being a "bad parent" and letting your bad day affect your child. Each time that a parent tells me about their yelling or their decision to punish because they couldn't take it anymore, I can hear the guilt and the shaming coming through in their voice. It sucks when your humanness bursts through the facade that as a parent you are a perfectly sane person with no room for intense emotions. We project because we have nowhere to throw our emotions. We have become accustomed to believing that intense emotions need to be stuffed in order to make our children come first in our lives. But stuffing these emotions is a great breeding ground for projection. Projection also rears its head when we are burned out, and especially when we scoff at self-care because we think that running on fumes makes us superhuman (yet another defense mechanism).

How to manage this defense mechanism:

When you recognize this parenting defense mechanism in your parenting, the best way to shame-proof it is to develop an empathy practice. We'll talk about developing an empathy practice when we get to the steps on how to begin shame-proofing your parenting. But, briefly, when you give yourself space to be human and express your emotions in a healthy way, you get better at recognizing when your child is needing that same space. This space can be time with close friends, commiserating with other parents, or even doing something that helps you get recharged.

Regression

Like projection, this is another defense mechanism that looks different for parents. Regression is when our behaviors reflect a past era in lives. Unfortunately, we don't tend to regress to the happier times; this is because our defense mechanisms come from times when we had to protect ourselves from something not so great! And your child's behavior will trigger the pieces of your human self that you've hidden (or thought that you'd hidden) through ignoring, forgetting, therapy, or any other healing strategy you've tried. Regression as a parenting defense mechanism, like watching your child display behavior that reminds you of that significant event, can bring you back to the coping strategies (or lack thereof) that you had at that difficult age. For example, if loud noises trigger you because as a child the chaos in your home kept you up at night, you might regress to that age when all you could do is try to ignore it and block it out—which means that when your child triggers you with irritating or annoying noise, you will regress to ignoring and shutting down instead of being able to guide your child.

How to manage this defense mechanism:

This parenting defense mechanism is one of the hardest to manage because it comes from a place that you most likely have tried to squash out of existence. Many of the traumatic or not so great events in our lives have caused us so much stress and pain, that we do a lot to shut it out. This makes it harder to retrieve and reflect on when we become parents. My encouragement for doing the work around this mechanism is to write out all the things that really get on your nerves now as a parent, whether it be your children or something else. Out of that list, search for a common theme. For example, after writing the list, you realize that many of the items fit under needing to be heard. Using this example, think about times in your childhood or early life where being heard was a desperate need that wasn't met. This need, that you've built a parenting defense mechanism around, is what now gets triggered whenever your child wants to be heard and you resent that you can actually give it to them when no one gave it to you. This example is on the surface, but it highlights how deep regression can go. This mechanism is oftentimes best addressed with more professional support, like a therapist, a coach, or an alternative healing professional.

> *Learn everything you can from the past, and then let it go. If earlier in your life others could not express their love to you it was because they were blocked, not because of some defect in you.*
>
> —Brian Weiss

Fear of failure

This one is more of a defense mechanism used to protect your parenting identity from the pain of failing yourself and others. Very rarely do parents use their actual family to help them understand how to move through making mistakes. Usually, it comes from what society says raising a child is and how the child is supposed to be by the end of their time with you. That's what parents generally measure themselves by. But this is really a defense.

Sounds crazy, right?

This fear of failure stops you from trying things and being okay with the trial and error aspect of being a parent, but it also shields you from judgment. It looks like this statement, "See I've done everything I was supposed to, so how my kid turns out is not my fault." It's almost like a defense that shifts blame and responsibility. It's a defense that allows parents to say that they gave the child everything, they made sure their child had sufficient opportunities, and it's the child's fault if he doesn't make something of that. It's very close to the martyr parenting defense mechanism we'll see next. The funny thing about this parenting defense mechanism is that while it shields you from the pain of failure, it also disconnects you from the reality of what's in front of you. When you stay in this fear, using this defense, you are not able to see the reality of what it means to be human, for yourself or for your child. You're not able to withstand the ebbs and flows of being human for fear that those ebbs and flows are going to make or break your identity. It's a defense that is detrimental to your whole parenting identity.

How to manage this defense mechanism:

This one is managed best by getting good at bringing to awareness what you are really afraid of, by being specific and not placing value on how fear shows up for you. If you're worried that you're going to be just like your parents, ask yourself why that scares you. If you're scared that your child will be a loser and never amount to anything, take stock of why you get to make that judgment of them. This fear is usually irrational and is driven by past trauma/negative experiences, and is rooted in shame/guilt. The only way to manage it is to bring it into reality and process the alternatives to it. You can do this by journaling, bringing those fears out of the messiness in your head and onto something tangible like paper, or by sharing your fears with your tribe of supportive friends who can give you the space to share, explore, and reflect on how your fears are showing up in your life. Another option is to get some professional support from a therapist, coach, or alternative healer.

Martyrdom

Martyrdom is when a parent sacrifices themselves in the hopes that the sacrifice will produce something for them, lives vicariously through their child for their own fulfilment, or takes a sacrifice that is detrimental to them in any way (physically, emotionally, mentally, financially) because it will benefit their child. It's a parenting defense mechanism that many parents use to justify the journey of raising a human. It's a parenting defense mechanism used to help parents manage the cognitive dissonance they experience, when they realize they've made a decision that may not have been for their child but was more for themselves. When we martyr ourselves under the myth of doing it for our child's well-being, we are setting the foundation for resentment that will turn into detachment from our child. Essentially, you're making your child pay for a decision they had no participation in. This parenting defense mechanism is hard to become aware of because most of your decisions about your child and your parenting are made with the best intentions.

How to manage this defense mechanism:

What I challenge when I see parents using this defense mechanism is to have them ask themselves: why did I just make that parenting decision?

Was it for me, for my child, for my parenting identity, or for something else? This question has to be answered authentically for you to be able to overcome this defense. Another way to combat this mechanism—especially if your child is old enough to discuss things with you—is to bring your child into any decision you'll be making that has an effect on who they are. For example, when you decide that your child is going to college and you do everything you can to make sure that he gets there, ask yourself why you are doing that. Then, include your teen in that discussion. If you spearhead getting them into college, with minimal effort or little to no input from your child, any decision your child makes about her college career that you don't love will cause you to build resentment for helping her get into college. Essentially, the most effective way to combat this defense mechanism is to bring your child into the equation when you're making decisions, so that you're not sacrificing your identity for something that your child won't want.

The Superhuman

This is a newer parenting defense mechanism that I have seen come up as a result of our culture's preoccupation with perfection and overdoing it. We seem to think that doing it all validates us and makes us a real human, while doing less than everything makes us less than and lazy. Being a superhuman is a myth that I constantly encourage my clients to rethink, as it breeds parents who are burned out, fatigued, and out of energy to do anything for themselves. I've seen parents be shamed for having nannies or live in sitters who help with the household, and I realize that this judgment comes from this parenting defense mechanism. I call it a defense because when you shame others who aren't as "busy," you create a barrier of inauthenticity and impossible expectations, as no human can truly do it all. Your children and others in your family begin to see you as superhuman, which initially feels great because your hard work is being acknowledged, but then turns to resentment as everyone in your family begins to dump all their stuff on you. Because they know you can take it.

Statistics[11] have shown that when a parent puts others' needs first, they are more likely to burn out, be more irritable, be more detached from their family, and be more resentful. This parenting defense mechanism is like the others in that it feels good in the short term, but in the long term it creates tension and disconnect.

How to manage this defense mechanism:

My go-to strategy for managing this parenting defense mechanism is to get to know yourself better. If you're doing everything to validate your value as a parent, trying to "Keep up with the Joneses," or simply wanting to make sure everyone in your family gets what they need, it all gets easier by knowing your worth, your needs, and how to be still in a world of chaos. Get to know yourself and your family, honoring each strength and each flaw. Being hard on yourself shuts down your self-empathy, which doesn't leave space to show empathy for your family. It's a vicious cycle that suppresses everyone. Try having conversations that have nothing to do with your to-do list, and instead ask about dreams, goals, tell jokes, and be silly—but don't judge, make fun of, or insult. Also, I encourage you to be honest about your abilities as you interact with other families and other parents. It's easy to get caught up in all the events that are occurring. Find solace in knowing that there are only so many hours in the day, and they don't all have to be filled up with activity. *Try saying no to some things, and don't feel pressured to put your child in everything.*

Now that you know what barriers will come up when you attempt to shame-proof your parenting—and they will come up—let's look at how to develop self-empathy to overcome those barriers. Every time you recognize your imperfections, you are getting closer to shame-proofing your parenting.

---

11   Morin, A. Do you have parental burnout?, 2008. Retrieved 2 February 2017, from https://www.education.com/magazine/article/Parental_Burnout/

Shame-proof parenting has nothing to do with perfection

[Parental burnout] often can start from a good place, such as wanting the best for children, but can head into feeling pressured to meet an impossible standard and/or pressuring children to meet impossible standards.

—Robin F. Goodman, PhD

Remember when we talked about parenting gimmicks and how they prey on the desperation that parent shaming has created in families? The concept of shame-proofing your parenting is not another technique that I want you to hold onto for dear life, and then reject when your child still has tantrums. It's not a strategy I want you to stand by blindly even when your intuition is telling you to just get on your child's level and connect with them. And it's not a piece of expert advice that only I can execute.

Shame-proofing your parenting is about giving you a framework to start looking at your parenting identity and your family as a whole, authentically imperfect system that needs connection, empathy, healing, and togetherness to heal, grow, and be healthy together.

Shame-proofing your parenting doesn't mean you won't explode or that things won't go wrong. But when the explosions happen, you will have the confidence, resilience, and know-how to manage the blast. When you shame-proof your parenting, the conflicts and the explosions won't burn everyone; you and your family will be protected from the burning shame by your own shame-proof encasing.

The gender divide in parent shaming

I know, I'm teasing you with the steps to shame-proofing your parenting in this chapter. But we have to talk about the underlying issues that stop the process of shame-proofing before we can talk about how to shame-proof. This discussion will help you be more aware of your parenting identity and how you created that identity, so you don't have the catastrophe of putting a Band-Aid over a bleeding wound.

With that said, let's talk about the gender divide in parenting. For the purposes of this book, we are looking at gender as both biological gender classifications and how you identify your own gender.

Women and mothers

One of the biggest issues I had with my own healing was deciding to walk away from the relationship with my mother (who, if you recall, is my step-grandmother). After the years of emotional abuse and the realization that she never truly wanted to be my mother—but did so out of obligation and a false sense of financial gain—I had to make the decision to choose my own healing and walk away from her and her matriarchal rule. The part that made it so difficult is that we put mothers on a pedestal that takes away their humanity and arbitrarily gives them power over their families. When I think about the title of mother, I see an exhausting role that takes away a woman's humanness in exchange for a larger than life presence in the raising of another human. It's that mental tug-o'-war that stops women from truly connecting to their humanness and truly connecting to what it means to be a fallible human who makes mistakes. When you detach from that humanness after taking on the mother title, it also detaches you from the human child that you are raising. It makes it hard to see that your role in their life is not to control or lasso, but to guide and nurture.

Mothers have a lot of pressure to be perfect, but no one tells them to be human. In our society, we revere mothers when they are doing what we think is right, but we demonize them when they do what we think is wrong. And in that flip flop of what we think is right or wrong (which seemingly changes with every generation), women are caught in the crosshairs struggling to find their true identity as a mother. They are forced to rely on what society says, because they have no space to cultivate an identity they want for fear that in the time it takes to cultivate a truly authentic and genuine mother identity, they will be shamed and judged for accidentally creating an asshole.

Take a look at that last sentence: can you imagine having that much pressure on you? Can you imagine why you create parenting defense mechanisms, ignore your intuition, and tightly grasp hold to whatever parenting strategy takes pressure off you? It's that pressure we put on women once they take on the mother title, that is a detriment to families and to healing for a family.

When I look at my decision to leave my mom, I know in my heart that it was a decision to heal me and not to demonize her. But because mothers are not allowed to be human, my doing this can be seen in our society as ungrateful (remember the martyr parenting defense mechanism), because a mother sacrifices for her child. How dare I ungratefully take that sacrifice and leave her? But outside of my own family drama, I see mothers all the time who, once they became a mom, constantly ignore so much of who they were. I usually ask my mothers this question: if this is the identity you developed and cultivated for about 20 years, what happens when that human goes off to live their life? This question is usually met with hesitation, confusion, guilt, sadness, and grief. Those emotions hurt me, because I know that the women who become mothers are told that leaving all their other identities behind to be a mom is how it is supposed to be. And the shame that gets thrown at women who refuse to stay in that box is unyielding.

The Dad Effect (revisited Under the Shame-Proof banner)

Things are not quite the same for men. The general idea is that a man is not supposed to be the nurturer or the caregiver; he is supposed to be the provider and the hunter-gatherer for the family. But that pressure is difficult to manage as well. As we all know, being a provider is just as burdened with pressure as is being a nurturer and the rock that holds the family together. And it's in that pressure that we fail men who become dads.

Taking a detour into my family drama again, I grew up with my grandfather being my dad, and my biological dad being in jail for hurting me as an infant. However, when I think back on the blame and shame that was thrown at my parental unit, it was mostly toward my biological mother for leaving me, and my step-grandmother for taking on too much by raising me. So, in essence, the men were able to sidestep the shame because the women were supposed to be the true caregivers.

But that silly notion backfires for the men who take the role of being a dad seriously. For every man that does not take on this role after bringing a child into the world, there is another man who does take on the role, and he must contend with the lack of empathy and support he needs to be the best he can in this role.

Seeing and hearing jokes about how kids need to go to mom instead of dad to get anything done, men babysitting their children, and the general disregard for the significance a man in his dad role provides for a family is disheartening. When people begin conversations about men being "men" and taking on their role as fathers, I reply with the same voracity I do when people bash women who take on the role of being a mom for their parenting choices. I ask, "How can a man be a father when there is no rule book or manual?"

We think there is a right or wrong way to parent, but there is not. And when we take these boxes (the provider, the babysitter, the loser who left) and try to fit every man into them, we discourage men from wanting to fully take on the role of dad, and we therefore deprive families of one of the crucial elements of being shame-proof: having the masculine influence to help build the shield around a family.

When I used to work with families in my community on mental health days, I remember talking to men (whether they were in their dad role or still struggling with that title), and each of them felt like being a father is not highly revered in this world, unless they were doing it "right." When I inquired about what "right" was, most of them laughed and threw up their hands in exasperation. No one truly knew what the right way to be a dad was, but they knew that they were going to try to be in their child's lives the best way they knew how.

I remember working with a father who constantly struggled with finding support in his community. He shared that before he became a father, he was known in the community as a drug dealer, and a pretty notorious one at that. But he explained that his whole perspective of life changed when his daughter came into his life and his daughter's mother left him as the sole caregiver. This father relayed the shame of his peers for taking on what they called "a woman's job," how he had to fight hard in court to be deemed appropriate when the mother's family said a man couldn't raise a girl, and even had to contend with his daughter's school, who asked him if there was a woman in his life to help care for his daughter. He lamented that this shame made him want to throw in the towel and just let the mother's family take his daughter. The only thing that kept him going was that his daughter told him that she preferred living with him and thought that he was the best dad in the world. He said that hearing this from his daughter helped shut out the noise of the world and the biases that were thrown at him simply because he was a man who dared to raise a daughter alone.

This father's story is unfortunately very familiar for men who decide to develop their parenting identity. And it's one that we must be aware of as we attempt to shame-proof our families.

In our culture, we do not take care, emotionally or mentally, of our men who take on fatherhood roles. While the emotional intelligence of men and boys is a whole other book topic, when it comes to the identity of being a father, it is crucial that we stop judging men for toughness and grit, and start allowing them to express their emotions in a way that is true and authentic to them. If you're a truly gritty, tough guy, be that way (and the same could be said for mothers who don't conform to female gender stereotypes of being touchy-feely and always emotional). But, if you're not, your manliness and title as father doesn't have to change to conform. And that is one of the most amazing things we can give our men who take on the role of being a father: the space to figure out what that role is, the time to develop that identity, and more room to make mistakes that don't have to be fixed by mom or the women in their lives.

Shame-proof our parenting: putting it all together

> *Pause before judging. Pause before assuming. Pause before accusing. Pause whenever you're about to react harshly and you'll avoid doing and saying things you'll later regret.*
>
> *—Lori Deschene*

And now, the meat of the meal: how the hell do you actually shame-proof your parenting?

As I stated earlier, these are not steps or strategies. Instead, I am presenting a framework that will create a shift in perspective in:

1. How you respond to yourself as a parent

2. Your relationship with your child

3. Your relationship with the people in your life who watch you parent

This framework has the benefit of being able to be executed with your own unique, authentic humanness, because when you decide to shame-proof your parenting, you're making a choice to change your parenting identity and how you connect to your family.

Without further ado—here is the Shame-Proof Parenting framework:

Empathy

Empathy is the key concept in shame-proofing your parenting. Without it, you cannot begin to connect with your family or collaborate on ways to manage conflict and behavior. In shame-proofing, empathy is being able to see another human as you see yourself (which is why healing, intuition, and understanding your story is an important pre-step to creating your shame-proof family). This means that you must understand that you are human and that you are fallible. Admitting this basic truth about yourself will also help you realize this for your child, and that sets the foundation for connection over punishment, action instead of reaction, and growth instead of stagnation.

Empathy is not permissiveness. When you give yourself or your child empathy, you are not saying it's okay that the event, behavior, or situation occurred and that you will just move on like it never happened. It means that you are open to finding out the motivations behind the behavior, because you know that all humans display behaviors as a way to achieve a goal, want, or need. You understand that there is no need to judge a person for wanting to have his or her needs met, but there is space for understanding the underlying actions that led to the behavior and looking at how we can find alternative, healthy options to have our needs met. Empathy will help you shame-proof your parenting, because it will help you connect with each other instead of detaching and using punishment and your parenting defense mechanisms to shield your family from the pain you are managing.

It's interesting to note that we often have so much empathy for people in every other relationship in the world, except the one between parent and child. I've shared earlier in the book that when we see people in other relationships or situations, we are apt to let them side step or exit the situation without much shame—but with parenting, where there literally is no way out, we box parents in with shame, guilt, and strategy. This is why I love using empathy as the first tenet of shame-proofing your parenting. When you're armed with this, especially with empathy for yourself above all, you begin to develop a shield to that shame and guilt, allowing yourself a space to reflect, grow, and find solutions.

Using this to shame-proof your parenting:

Empathy can be used even when you do not have all the parenting tools that you need, even if the day has been so hectic that you couldn't find time for self-care, and even when your child is having a difficult time managing their feelings. When you use empathy to guide your actions, you don't just react to what you see your child doing. You can take a step back and get a bigger view of what may be causing your child to feel a certain way, or to display a certain behavior. And you allow a space that says, although I am not happy with my child's behavior, I will take the time to be curious about what's going on for them.

But, let's be real, empathy can be a difficult concept when we are stretched thin and running out of fuel. Empathy asks us to hold a space for the other person, but what about holding a space for yourself? It's in that question that we learn to value and develop true empathy. This is because giving empathy starts from within. You have to give yourself empathy when you are not able to get all the things on your to-do list completed, or when you forget to pack your child's lunch, or when you mix up your days and over-schedule yourself. Allow yourself the space to say, "I am here, in the space, in this place, right now. And wherever it is, it's okay." It can be so liberating to be able to give yourself empathy and to see how calming it is to know that you are where you are, and that's okay.

Now, when you've given yourself that space, you can begin to see your child's behavior in a different light. For example, instead of seeing your child's tantrum as a wrench in your plans, you can see that your child is having big emotions because a need was not met. Or, another example could be that instead of being frustrated with your teen for not getting their homework done, you can be curious about what barrier may be causing them to have trouble with their school work. These perspectives don't come easy, but when we practice empathy, the way we see ourselves and our children changes. We have more space to be curious and less space to be judgmental. We have more time to say, "What happened to you today?" as opposed to saying, "What the heck is wrong with you?"

Awareness

Awareness is going to be your most formidable tool in your shame-proofing parenting tool box. When you think about all the recovery type programs for getting over addiction and healing, what's the first step? Admitting that there is a problem. The awareness that something is amiss leads people on the path to recovery and eventual healing. If awareness can do that for healing addiction, what do you think it can do for your parenting and your family?

The good news about awareness is that it is not about blame, so you don't have to point the finger to get to awareness. But you can begin to see that something isn't going the way you want in your parenting and in your family. When we are in conflict, this is the perfect time to stop and become aware—not to react and punish. Conflict will always be an awareness alert. Conflict says, "Hey something is wrong here, something is not working here." Again, that does not mean react, that means stop and take stock of the situation.

Remember when we talked about intuition? That's your internal way of bringing awareness to your life. Intuitive awareness is usually preceded by external awareness (or external conflict). When something feels off in your gut, especially when it pertains to your parenting choice or your child, it usually is. Taking that awareness and getting quiet, you can usually find the root cause of the intuitive nudge. When I've asked parents to spend a week not punishing but just connecting, they have come back saying that they were able to figure out what was going on under their child's behavior, AND they were able to reduce conflicts. Why? Because they helped their child through the moment as opposed to punishing their child for something.

Using this to shame-proof your parenting:

One of the best ways to use awareness in your shame-proof parenting is to get curious. Instead of assuming that you know why and what, ask more questions to get a more in-depth understanding of what's going on in your child's head and what her motivations were. When we go right into lecturing or punishing because we assume we know why, we shut our children down and they begin to defend and protect themselves rather than reflect and grow from their decisions. Curiosity also gives you a better direction of where to guide your child. When you assume, you make a blanket decision on what lesson your child needs to learn. But when you get curious and ask open-ended questions, you get more information on your child's thinking and processing, leading you to the best lesson to teach your child in that moment.

Now, I know what you're thinking: what if my intuitive awareness tells me what's going on? That's a great question, and I'll pat you on the back for creativity. But here's how you use that intuition: to direct the open-ended questions you ask. If your intuitive awareness is saying your child is using marijuana, use that intuitive knowledge to ask about why he used it, what was he trying to do, what need was he trying to get met, what goal did he meet, and did he get what he was looking for? You see, the intuitive awareness will help you get into your child's thinking so you can help them get what they need in another, healthier way!

Knowing what you need

Needs assessment is something that is the backbone of all healing, and it's going to be one of the pillars of shame-proofing your parenting. Remember when we distinguished needs versus wants earlier in the book? You can't know how to check in with what your child needs unless you know what *you* need. Even if you can't get that need met right now, you should know what your needs *are* in order to meet them as soon as you can.

When you know what you need, you can give yourself empathy for needing, rather than guilt, and you can bring awareness to how you are meeting that (or how you are avoiding having it met). This concept leads us directly to self-care. Everyone needs it, but most parents shuck it as a luxury.

You are not required to set yourself on fire to keep others warm.

—Unknown

I have met so many parents who use the martyr parenting defense mechanisms as a barrier to them knowing what they need, and subsequently in meeting those needs. The backfire here is that because you don't truly know what you need, or you refuse to acknowledge that you have needs, you detach from that piece of your parenting identity, and you cannot connect with your child's attempts to get his own needs met. It frustrates you to see your child doing disruptive things in pursuit of his needs, because you have ignored the things you do to meet your own. You yell to get the room clean because you have a need for cleanliness. You give timeouts because you have a need for quiet in your home. You spank or tap on the hand because you are frustrated and no one seems to know that. All these needs are important, and giving space to what you need is integral to shame-proofing your parenting.

Using this to shame-proof your parenting:

When you get good at identifying your needs, you begin to shame-proof your parenting from parenting defense mechanisms and external forces that cause you to detach from your needs, and force you to get your needs met in maladaptive ways. The best way to identify your own needs is to have a list of needs that all humans have. See the Needs Inventory checklist. This inventory not only brings common needs into the forefront of your mind, but it also alerts you to needs that we commonly have but don't always have the words to express. When we are able take this into account, we set the foundation for shame-proofing our families to withstand the external forces that push against us.

Confidence

Somewhere along the way, we started interchanging arrogance with confidence, that if we are confident in something, it must mean that we are arrogant know-it-alls who have no space to grow. But confidence and arrogance are two different things. Confidence is a belief that you are good at something or that you can do something well. This definition and the admittance that you are confident, helps you shame-proof your parenting, because it makes it difficult for something to come knock you off your game when you make a mistake.

Parent shaming works so well because many parents believe that they are failing at parenting. And that may be true for some aspects of your parenting journey. Failing is a part of any endeavor, and because you are human and not perfect, there will be some areas of parenting in which you will not do well, which is actually a good thing. Trying to do it all well makes you a jack of all trades and master of nothing. As you'll be learning in the support section below, being good at a few things in your parenting allows you to reach out for support in other areas where you struggle.

Therefore, think of what areas of your parenting you are confident in, and take pride in the spaces where you do well. Let's say, for example, that you're really good at packing nutritious lunches, or you're really organized, or you're really great at coming up with creative ways to play during snow days, or you're good at advocating for your child at school. I want to encourage you to get away from the notion that you don't need to highlight your strengths because you're just doing what any parent would do, or you feel like it would sound selfish to assume that you're doing well at something. In our haste to be self-deprecating and have that "we're all in the same struggle" ideology, we forget that we each have a uniqueness that we bring to our parenting identities. Essentially, finding your strengths allows you to be confident that the things you do or accomplish in your family, are what keep your family afloat.

On that same note, I want you to think about the things that people tend to tease you or shame you about. For example, if you're constantly being told you're a helicopter parent, you can reframe that as a strength of being a safety net for your children to practice limits and learn boundaries. Or, if you've been told that you advocate too much for your child, you can reframe it as being able to see parts of your child that others don't always get to see. The idea here is to reframe those things that others use to shame or guilt you into a strength. When you do this, you're able to reflect on what you're doing as opposed to being defensive about it, and you can find ways to make it a strength for your parenting. Finding your strengths allows so much more space for learning and growing than constantly berating yourself, being self-deprecating, or even getting defensive when things are brought up that you're sensitive about.

Measure this confidence with what you and your family need, not with what society says you should be confident in. And while you're at it, please do not start diving into the spaces where you do not do well. We have an uncanny affinity as humans to ignore the many good things we do well, for the one thing we don't do well. That's the biggest killer to your confidence for a parent: only focusing on the not so great things you do. It's not about being Zen or being kumbaya about it. Confidence in your parenting is not about ignoring your imperfections. Instead, it's about realizing that your failures and your successes are not mutually exclusive—they can exist at the same time. That truth is relevant for your parenting as well. You can be great at creating space for your child to talk to you and not so great at setting limits; you can be great at setting limits, and really not so good at being flexible. Be confident in what you're good at; then, look at where you can get support for the areas where you aren't as confident!

Using this to shame-proof your parenting:

Allowing yourself to be confident in some area allows your child to be confident in some areas too. It's a domino effect: when you feel confident in yourself, you have more space for your child's successes and more empathy for their failures. You know that no one can be good at everything, and since you don't place that expectation on yourself, you don't place it on your child. When external influences try to force you and your family into that arrogance/ego box, suggesting you think you know it all or that your child is full of himself for being confident, you can use that shame-proof shield to correct them on what confidence is and how integral it is to your family's overall health.

Resilience

Resilience has been a buzzword in the self-help, mental health, emotional health world for a long time. The idea is that with resilience, we are able to bounce back when things get tough. But using resilience to shame-proof your parenting is about helping you and your family be more flexible with one another, and to be more elastic with each other and yourself so your family doesn't break under pressure. When you bring resilience to your parenting, you can stretch past what you thought you could handle with your family, and expand the ways in which your family can manage situations. When you decide that there is only one way to handle a tantrum, or one strategy to communicate with each other, you're making things so rigid that when something comes barreling fast at your family, you break. That constant breaking detaches you from your parenting, brings up those pesky parenting defense mechanisms, and stops you from connecting. But with resilience, you can expand past what you initially thought possible with your family's coping and together build more strategies to manage issues.

Using this to shame-proof your parenting:

For a shame-proof family, your resilience will make it a lot harder for externally forced shame and guilt to mess with your parenting identity, giving you more space to connect with your family and heal together. This elasticity comes from allowing the other aspects of shame-proofing your parenting to manifest in your parenting. For example, when you bring resilience to your parenting, you have more reserves to manage conflict, which gives more space to figure out what needs are not being met. Thus, in shame-proof parenting, being resilient isn't just about bouncing back, it's also about being able to withstand external pressure by letting positive attributes like awareness, empathy, support, and confidence be the ingredients to managing what comes against you and your family.

Support

Support is to shame-proof parenting as a foundation is to a house. Without the right base, your home will fall at the slightest blow from the big bad wolf. Support becomes those beams and those structural supports that help bolster your parenting. But how do we get support?

The unfortunate thing is that shame, societal prescriptions on what parenting is, and parenting defense mechanisms can be a barrier to receiving support. Common parenting sense dictates that you should know how to do everything your child needs, and that is preposterous. When you're on the path to shame-proofing your parenting, support is crucial because you cannot do everything, and confidence, along with knowing what you need, will be integral in knowing how to seek support.

A shame-proof parent who has support will be able to get the help they need, while simultaneously shielding their family from judgment. A shame-proof parent knows that they cannot do it all alone, and they allow their support system to help them even as the internal whispers try to shame them into keeping silent about needing help.

Another aspect of support is knowing that it's there in the background, even when you're confident that you can manage things yourself. This goes back to the necessity of self-care; just because you can do it and do it confidently, doesn't mean you have to burn yourself out doing it all the time. For example, you might love cleaning your house and you might be very good at it. But there are definitely times when it would be nice to have someone else do it; so, hire out. Or you have nothing scheduled—no work, no client, no appointment—but you really need a break to just sleep; so, get a babysitter for a few hours. Part of support is knowing when you need support, and that includes when you need support for self-care.

Using this to shame-proof your parenting:

In the confidence section, I talked about knowing what you're good at. By knowing this, you can seek out the support for the things that you are not good at. For example, you might hire a tutor for your child in math because you know that math is not your strongest ability. The same can be done when it comes to other aspects of our parenting. If you're not good at setting limits, it doesn't make you a bad parent; it makes you a human who can't do everything. So, you get support for how to set limits (hence the parenting strategies, experts, and coaching). Without knowing what you're good at, it's hard to know what to ask for support with.

Your unique parenting manual

Yes! This is the part of shame-proofing your parenting that will help you transcend external forces and be consistent in your connection with your child. The most basic skills you need reside in knowing your family and what they need to feel connected and to be authentically human. This requires you to shame-proof your parenting. If you're spending all your time hiding behind your parenting defense mechanisms, focusing on generic parenting strategies, and defending your parenting choices, you have no time to get to know your children and to use parenting tools that are in alignment with who they are.

Your unique parenting manual is essentially all the tools you use to connect with your child, get to know them, and help them come to terms with the fallacy of being a human.

So much of what current parenting trends are telling us, is that we're setting our kids up to be conscious and healthy, but the unfortunate part is that no matter how well you parent your child or how much you try to be conscious, you are still human and there are times when your conscious parenting skills fall flat. We are unconscious beings sometimes, running on fumes and just trying to get by; we make mistakes and we are not perfect. Shame-proofing you parenting helps give your family the space to heal and recover from this, under the protection of love and connection.

When you use *your* parenting manual, instead of someone else's, the life blood of who you are and who your children are pulses through the strategies you choose. You pick the strategies that work for your family in the present, and you continue to use the shame-proof shield you've created to reassess and reevaluate what those strategies are as you all grow and evolve.

Thus, your unique parenting manual is a living, breathing experience rather than a stagnant set of tools. You will be adapting this manual through the course of your parenting journey—just as you will always be your child's parent—even once your child has children. It's in realizing this truth that you will be able to maintain that shame-proof armor. You get to make mistakes, trial and error, and grow as a human at the same time your child is making mistakes, learning from them, and being human. It's a parallel experience that is difficult at times and beautiful at others. But it is the best way to shame-proof your parenting, because it allows you to feel free to explore and grow.

Conclusion

Shame-proof parenting is not another set of parenting concepts that you must remember and get right. It is the road map for being more authentic, allowing your child to be human, and letting this awareness envelope you and your family against a world that demands perfection. Living an authentic life might sound like a bunch of bologna when all you want to do is know for a fact that you are not raising a horrible human. But how can you know that you're raising a healthy kid if you're not sure what that looks like for yourself? Shame-proofing comes from modeling the ebbs and flows that come with navigating this world, and from bringing concepts like resilience, support, awareness, and empathy to the forefront of your parenting decisions, instead of always jumping to the disciplinary tactics. But I'm no fool, I know that shame-proofing your parenting is a journey—not a destination!

SHAME-PROOF, NOT BULLET-PROOF

The irony is that we attempt to disown our difficult stories to appear more whole or more acceptable, but our wholeness—even our wholeheartedness—actually depends on the integration of all of our experiences, including the falls.

—Brené Brown

Now that the fun part is over, let's get real! Being shame-proof is great for the times when everyone is happy and things are going well. But what about the times when your child is really showing his not-so-wonderful side? What happens when you've tried to keep the shame-proof parenting mindset and your child still throws a tantrum? Or what about when you've been burning the candlestick at both ends and you're just too burned out to be as present as you'd like to? It's in these times that shame can creep in and knock you off your shame-proof parenting journey. Now that you have the shame-proof parenting framework, let's take a look at how to apply this to real life situations in your family.

Now, here's the cycle that I see all the time in parents who attempt to bring any type of parenting philosophy or parenting strategy into their lives:

Get frustrated, search for something that will stop whatever is stressing them in their parenting or with their child, attempt to implement, get hung up in all the minutia of it, lose hope because it doesn't work, get frustrated.

Rinse and repeat.

This cycle happens because it's easy to forget that being a parent is a fluid experience. It's not something that has a fixed set of steps. And when trying to implement someone else's framework, we forget that we are constantly being influenced by the ever-changing world that both you and your children live in.

This is why shame-proofing is a framework, not a step-by-step process. It's a belief that you are human, and your child is human. And that the best way to help manage all that humanness is to connect with each other by providing a force field that protects you all long enough to recover and repair, and get back to being a functioning family unit.

If you noticed, I said a "functioning family unit." I make this distinction because I know how tempting it is to be so overwhelmed with the stress of raising healthy kids that you want everything to work perfectly. Can't they just go to sleep so I can get some work done? What's the issue with getting along—I thought they were siblings, not dueling countries? If you've ever asked yourself questions like this, then I know that simply functioning feels like lowering your expectations for your family.

Let me reframe the idea of a functioning family unit. A shame-proof family is a family that is growing together and is definitely *not* without conflict. The shame-proof parent and family is one that still has conflict, but that conflict does not undo all the connection and relationship building that has been developed over the years. So, if your family is functioning, that means that you are at least working together to get things done and move through life—and that's what the goal is in shame-proof parenting.

The truth is this: you cannot control the influences in the world. You cannot control how traffic or co-workers will affect you. You cannot control how school and peers will affect your children. You cannot control how people's opinions of your family will affect you. But you know what you can influence: the space you create in your home to regroup.

Let's look at a few things that can help, and some things that can be a huge barrier to maintaining that shame-proofing for you and your family.

Honesty is the best policy

How many times do you tell your child not to lie? And how upset are you when your child attempts to escape punishment by lying? Being dishonest is the best way to disconnect from someone and make them question everything you say to them. But what about when you lie? What about when you say you are too tired to play when you obviously have energy to read a book? I know parents sometimes lie (you might even call them white lies) to soften the blow of reality for their children or to keep their children in an age-appropriate understanding of life. And sometimes you lie because you don't want to tell the truth for whatever reason. But if you agree with the sentiment that lying creates a barrier in a relationship, then think about how your children feel when they've realized that you lied to them.

The most effective way to maintain your shame-proofing is to be honest with each other. About feelings. About events. About ideas. About failures. About successes. About things that affect the family.

Too many times, I see parents keep kids in the dark because they feel that their child is not ready to hear about what's going on in the family. While I agree that there are things that are not age appropriate for a child to know, here's a rule of thumb: if it's going to affect how I react, attend to, and connect with my child, I should talk to them about it.

> When we talk to our children, our words are seeds. We may not see what we have planted for years to come. Be wise with your words. No one likes to grow weeds.
>
> —Nastasha Daniels

Many of the times that you are struggling to talk to your child about something, it's more about your comfort level than theirs. I have sat in on so many sessions where I help a parent find the words to talk to their child about an issue that caused a rupture in their relationship, only to realize that the more they explain the situation to their child, the more empathy their child has for them. If you don't believe me, think about how helpful you are when your child tells you that they have homework but they really hate doing it, as opposed to telling you that they don't have homework. The same thing happens when you talk to your children honestly.

For example, one of the major things that shakes up a family is a divorce. I've worked with so many families where the main ruptures and problem behaviors stem from how the parents have kept major details about the separation from the child, sometimes in an effort to spare them the pain of knowing what a parent did, or what occurred in the relationship. Now, I know that this is a touchy subject. But in terms of being honest, here's how you can shame-proof your family: ask your child what they would like to know about the separation. This open-ended question allows your child to lead the discussion instead of you trying to cherry pick what you think they should hear. If your child asks a question that is tough, messy, or not age appropriate, let them know that it is a tough, mess, not age-appropriate topic. This level of honesty actually helps children create whole stories around what happens in their families, which allows for healing later on in life, versus creating stories with gaps they fill with assumptions. On the whole, simply asking what they'd like to know, helps bypass the unconscious conflicts and behaviors in your family.

When you shame-proof your family, it doesn't mean that things won't come against you, and coping in a healthy way with how to talk about difficult situations is vitally important. The knee-jerk reaction in these situations, which is to lie, can really be a burden on families. When trying to manage the influence that external forces have on your family, being honest yourself sets a model for your child to come to you to be honest, too.

There are few things worse than when a child can tell that their parent is lying. A lot of the bad behaviors I observe come from kids who don't trust that their parents are going to follow through on promises, or aren't going to tell them the truth. The behavior is a way for them to protect themselves from the frustration and pain of having to watch you not tell them the truth again. Does that motivation for behavior sound familiar to you? (Hint: parenting defense mechanisms.)

Learning how to manage and talk about fears and anxiety

We've talked a lot about finding your awareness, listening to your intuition, managing your parenting defense mechanisms, and shame-proofing your parenting. And I know that's all well and good, but when fear or anxiety kicks in, all that stuff goes right out the window. That's why I wanted to talk to you about how to manage it so that it doesn't shatter the shame-proof filter that you've created for your family.

So, here's the long and short of it, when the fears and anxieties come up, think of it this way: You are in your child's life to help them be better humans who can function in life without constant surveillance.

But you might ask yourself: "What if they fail? What if they get hurt? What if they don't succeed?"

Well, that's part of life. I know, a bit glib. How can you just let your child fail and not succeed, especially when you have the answers for how they cannot fail?

Here's how: You help your child be their best by giving them the tools they will need to cope with life's disappointments and frustrations. We talked about this earlier in the book when I asked you to meditate on the question of what tools you want your child to have by the time they turn 18 years old.

You know why this is the way to truly help your child? Because no matter how much you hate to see your child suffer, they will sometimes have difficult times. There is no way on earth that you can stop your child from having hard times.

Let's move the focus from your child to you. How many times in your life have you failed, not succeeded, made a mistake, made the wrong choice? I bet as you begin to think about that, you're also hoping that you can save your child from making similar mistakes. But here's the rub: you can save your child from what you know, but that just sends them on another path that neither of you have walked down, a path that is fraught with highs and lows, ups and downs, and successes and failures.

> *Instead of saying "I'm damaged, I'm broken, I have trust issues," say "I'm healing, I'm rediscovering myself, I'm starting over."*
>
> *—Horacio Jones*

I'm not saying to just let your child make mistakes and hope that they are insightful enough to reflect and grow from them. I am telling you that when fear shows up, think back on shame-proofing your family. If you take the time to shame-proof, you can be the one who guides your child to the learning they need to develop the insight to turn mistakes and failures into lessons that will help them succeed next time.

Let's dig a bit deeper: most of your fears and anxieties come from you, what you know and have experienced, and what others have shamed or fear mongered you into thinking. Very little of what you are anxious about in your child is coming from what you know about them—the connection that you have with them—or the time you've spent getting to know how they process and grow from life. As I've walked you through this whole book, we've talked about shame and how it weaves into how we react and perceive our parenting and our relationship with our children. That same idea applies to letting fear/anxiety dictate how you guide your children.

So, I challenge you to stop with the "I just want to protect them" or "I don't want anything to happen to them" mindset because it's those thoughts that will prevent you from preparing your child with the tools they will need to live their life away from you!

When those thoughts do come up, use them to bolster and strengthen your shame-proof parenting; use them as your shame-proof shield! Help your child by teaching them what fear is, by naming it when it comes up for you. Instead of yelling all the time, sit your child down and say:

"I stopped you from doing XYZ because I was afraid that you would get hurt/ fail/be sad/etc."

And then, here's the fun part: listen to how they respond to that statement. Listen when your child tells you that they want to try, or that they want to do something scary. Of course, use your best judgment, but at the same time, let them experience what things feel like with the safety of your support.

Here's a snapshot of what that looks like: Your tween has packed her schedule way too full, in your opinion, and you want her to drop something. When you bring this up to her, she exclaims that she'll be fine and that she really wants to try this schedule. At this point, every aspect of your being is telling you that she's either going to fail her classes or do really poorly in one of her extracurricular activities. You can foresee this, but she cannot, and you really need her to know that this schedule is not in her best interest. What are you supposed to do?

It's discussion time.

You check in with what you notice in her behavior as the time goes on, and have discussions about how she's doing well handling her schedule and where some things are slipping through the cracks. You manage your anxiety by checking in regularly, but also by listening to how she is processing her own schedule. You share with her your fears, but you also leave space for her to share her fears. You brainstorm solutions with her and let her try it out. And you also take stock of how you live your life to see where she may be getting the idea that a packed scheduled is something to aspire to. It's moments like this that allow her to learn from her decisions while you remain a guide for her to find healthy solutions.

In this moment, it's more important to listen to where your child is at so you can redirect that fear/anxiety into a problem-solving experience with your child. You can be a safety net for your child (giving them space to try, fail, learn, and try again), you can teach instead of judge (with the ability to teach your children how to fail and recognize the emotions that come up from failure), and you can create a space to role model what it means to work through fear and failure (by naming it and letting your child in on your process, you get to give them a bird's eye view of how this looks, beginning to end).

A shame-proof parent doesn't ignore or stop the fear and anxiety that comes up for you as you raise your child. Instead, manage what you expect of yourself and what you expect of your child, so that your child truly understands what it means to be a human. Fear and anxiety is normal—it's a part of the human process—but when a shame-proof parent comes up against it, they approach it with empathy, reflection, and guidance. And in those moments, when it's too intense and too difficult to meet it with these traits, name that too, and name it with your support systems (which we'll talk about in the next chapter) so that you're not managing this alone.

When emotions run high

This is the one piece of being a human that no amount of parenting strategy can prepare you for. But that's why the idea of shame-proofing your parenting is so useful. In shame-proofing your parenting, you are becoming aware of the humanness that comes with living and being a parent, so much so that emotions do not bring up shame. Instead, they cause you to lean into those emotions. What I mean is this: when emotions run high in a shame-proof family, they don't shame one another for having normal reactions to situations. They empathetically respond to each other and give each other the space to feel, be human, and work through the temporary occurrence of emotions.

Emotional intelligence is not simply about naming and identifying emotions; it's about being okay with emotions, even when they are intense. It's the understanding that emotions are temporary, real for the person experiencing them, and very much a part of how we live in the world. You are not wrong as a parent for having emotions, especially when your child triggers you. But the same is true for your child: they get triggered as well. In shame-proofing your parenting, you are helping reduce the shame that usually comes with experiencing human emotions.

I once worked with a family who had a young son they described as sensitive. Both Mom and Dad were getting frustrated with their child because he was constantly bothered by everything in his environment and couldn't go a whole day without having several meltdowns. When I inquired about the limit they had set for having emotional experiences, they looked at me awestruck. The idea that they could give their child space to feel had never crossed their mind. They explained that they spent most of their time trying to stop him from feeling so much, so he wouldn't be so triggered by everything. I suggested that they set up a space in the house where their son could go when he was feeling any emotion, and in that space, he was the leader, he could ask for support from mom or dad, or he could use that space to feel what he needed to feel. This space was not punishing him for feeling, but rather honoring his emotional experiences by giving them their own sacred space. This works for us all because when we get space to have big feelings, we eventually learn how to manage them by learning what these emotions feel like in our bodies.

The good news is, every time you resist acting on your anger and instead restore your calm, it gets easier. In fact, neurologists say you're actually rewiring your brain to be calmer and more loving.

—Dr. Laura Markham

I can tell you that conflict and intense emotions will happen in your family, even if you make the choice to walk the journey of shame-proofing your family. Like the title of the chapter suggests, you will not be immune to issues and conflict. But by looking at your emotions as normal and temporary, and giving your child the same respect, you get to harness the power that comes with shame-proofing your family, to create a safe haven for your family against the society that says that emotions have to be controlled. You get to show yourself and your child that every human has emotions, and that it's how we learn to express and discuss our emotions that both creates barriers and builds relationships.

I'll venture even further into this, because I know that it can be difficult experiencing intense emotions yourself and definitely can be tough when your child is experiencing them. I can also hear you saying as you're reading this that I don't know your child and how intense they can get. And you'd be right, I don't know you or your child. But I know what it means to be a human. And I know that no matter the diagnosis, the event, or the personality, emotions are always temporary and can be managed best with empathetic support, without shame, and without being made to feel like an oddity because you feel strongly. That truth is something that I have come to find out as a human myself, and it's one that has resonated for all the parents I work with. No one wants to be identified solely by their emotional makeup. Each of us is worthy of empathetic support, even when we haven't done the best at expressing ourselves.

Part of shame-proofing your parenting is getting good at understanding that you are worthy of being emotionally human. Before you can even share that empathy with others, you have to give yourself that space. This empathy evolves out of owning your story and honoring your experiences, so you can begin to understand where it was in your life that you took on the idea that emotions were bad, burdensome, or bothersome. Finding that piece for yourself can truly help you shame-proof your family from making that same conclusion about emotions.

Shame-proofing your parenting does not mean that you and your child will not butt heads emotionally. But it does give you some foundation to move through those difficult times together, and come out on the other end with more insight into yourselves, allowing you to navigate similar emotions and experiences in the future with less tension.

Why family meetings matter

Every family that I start seeing has to do a family meeting in the beginning. Their sole purpose is to get the family talking again. I don't care if it's chaotic or messy, I just want the family to start talking to each other. As we begin to tease out the concerns and themes that are brought up in each meeting, all of my families start to see what's really going on— everything from true feelings about one another, revelations about events each member has encountered and endured, and realization about how they communicate come up. These meetings provide a great revelation for a family to see where there are barriers, and actually hear each other's perspectives about what those actual barriers are.

You might be thinking that you already know where your family has barriers. But when it comes to shame-proofing your parenting, you have to do away with all of your assumptions and biases.

Family meetings challenge you to do some reality checking, which is testing the running narrative each family member has in their heads with what's actually happening. Too many times, I see families disconnect, not solely because of behaviors and conflicts, but because each family member decides that they know the motivations and reasons for the other members' behaviors. That starts a cycle of not talking because they already know how it will play out. This is why family meetings are so important. They take everyone out of their rehearsed mental scripts and force them into reality.

This process is especially moving for parents who sometimes forget that the person they're raising is a living, breathing, thinking, feeling human who also has ideas about what's going on in the family, and whose behaviors are a reflection of how this child has learned to survive in their family. This truth is evident when I get parents to talk about their family of origin and realize that many of them did the same thing in their own families. By the time they were old enough to notice things, they had already created survival behaviors to navigate the messiness of their family. When you shame-proof your family, family meetings help you to stop the cycle of assumptions, and help you and your family learn how to work together.

Choose feelings over logic, adventure over perfection, here over there, now over then, and always love, love, love.

—From "Notes From The Universe"

But here's the caveat: not all issues will be resolved in one family meeting. Shame-proofing does not mean that you or your family will get to the bottom of an issue quickly. Some issues are quickly resolved by clearing up a misunderstanding or letting someone vent. But larger issues in a family—ones that have been brewing for a while—take time to come to the surface. In those instances, the shame-proofing reveals itself in the patience you have with one another to move to a resolution. One person may hold on to something longer than the other person, but that's not an abnormal response to an issue that hurt them greatly. And just as having empathy for emotions is important, holding space for each person to move through an issue in their own time is one of the pillars of shame-proofing. You're teaching your child that they have worth, that their pain and their feelings are worthy and that they don't have to get over it just because everyone else has.

The best example I have seen of this playing out was with a dad learning that he had more value in his family than he thought. This dad came to family meetings feeling like he didn't have a lot to add to the family, because he worked a lot and the mom usually took care of things in the house. What came out of the family meetings was that he felt his ideas about child-rearing were constantly overshadowed by mom's ideas. So, slowly over the years, he just stopped trying to have ideas. During his work with me and his commitment to the family meetings, he began to see his children taking his suggestions and the mom even stepped back a bit to let dad facilitate meetings. This took time, as Dad would sometimes not show up to the meetings for fear he would be left out of the problem solving of the family, since he was at work when certain events took place. But I coached the family to have more patience with him as he learned to find his confidence. In this example, the dad found that his family appreciated his role in the family as both a provider and as someone who had quick, logical solutions to their issues.

Yes, this can be hard to work through. And that's why I'm talking about it here. The shame-proof concept is about creating a space and shield for healing, reflecting, and growth. And even if you're shaking your head, saying that you're not a therapist or healer, that's not what I'm encouraging you to be. When you shame-proof your parenting, you are saying that you want to reduce shame for the humanness that does not go away just because you are a parent. You are still human underneath your parenting title, and the same goes for your child. Even though they are developing and they are in your care, they are still human too, and when you reduce shame for yourself, you also reduce shame for them. They get to live in a space with you that shows them what it looks like to feel less shame and to cope with shame when others throw it at them. That's what you're doing in your family meetings. You're creating that space where shame cannot exist, because your family is allowing you to just be.

I always give my families a template for how to hold a family meeting, even if they've had them in the past, just to help the flow of the meeting.

Family meeting template

When I work with my families, this is the template that I use to help them get started. The only instruction I give them is to just do it, to not worry about the messiness of it or how many people attend. Just get in the habit of holding the meetings at least once a week. When time issues come up, ask yourself how important it is to have space for your family to connect, versus how important it is to do that task that is taking you away from the meeting. I challenge my families to make it a weekly appointment for at least one month before they give up on it. The cool thing that I've seen happen is that families are usually so desperate for that connection that after a month, even if it's been hard to coordinate, they keep doing it, or they at least attempt to make time for it bi-weekly or monthly.

To use this template, simply print it out or make a copy and set a date. If your family is not used to meeting together, I'll even suggest that you buy actual invitations (don't print out computer ones, actually get real invitations), and give every family member an invite to this meeting.

Family Meeting Template

Doing family meetings are a great way to create a safe space for everyone in the family to express themselves and problem solve together as a family!

The template is a way to get started with your family meetings, but please feel free to change it up and go with what your family needs as you get more comfortable doing these meetings!

Topics Addressed

Strengths / Positives:

Meeting Date:

Barriers / Challenges:

Meeting Facilitator:

Meeting Theme:

Solutions Found To Barriers:

Duration of Meeting:

Family Members Present:

NOTES

Meeting Date:

Rupture and repair cycle

In Japan, broken objects are often repaired with gold. The flaw is seen as a unique piece of the object's history, which adds to its beauty. Consider this when you feel broken.

—Unknown

In Dr. Dan Siegel and Mary Hartzell's amazing book, *Parenting From The Inside Out*, they talked about the rupture and repair cycle that happens in all relationships, but specifically in the parent-child relationship.[12] This cycle is something that is inevitable and common for your relationship with yourself and with your child.

The rupture and repair cycle happens when there are breakdowns in communication such as arguments, disagreements, conflicts, and not seeing eye-to-eye with each other—and then taking steps to repair that communication breakdown. In this cycle, what I see happening so much is that we take conflict personally, which causes us to disconnect from the person we have a conflict with, in this case our children, and that stops the process of repairing. What happens even further is that in many families' ruptures happen over and over again, but do not get repaired because of our inability to not take things personally.

But let's not go down the negative path here. Ruptures happen, that's certain. But repairs in a shame-proof family help us reconnect and get through the issue together.

The repair part of this cycle goes beyond apologizing, even though that

---

12   Hartzell, M. & Siegel, D. Parenting from the inside out: How a deeper self-understanding can help you raise children who thrive (1st ed.), 2005. New York: J.P. Tarcher/Penguin.

helps. It reaches into understanding what caused the conflict and how it affected all those involved. Becoming shame-proof helps bridge the gap. If you're viewing your parenting decisions through the shame-proof parenting framework, then the repair part will occur.

But just as I said regarding the above concepts, repairing doesn't happen overnight. It definitely can, but it doesn't always. This is especially true when there have been years of ruptures in your family. No matter how much you commit to shame-proofing your parenting, you're going to have to do some repair. Most parents take a good look at their parenting when conflict and problem behaviors exceed their normal set of coping skills. All the parenting strategies you have, all the coping skills you've developed will usually help you get through some of your child's early behaviors. But the way to continuously move through and shame-proof your parenting permanently is to get good at leaning into the rupture and repair cycle.

I mentioned earlier that this cycle happens in you, as well. When you are shamed by a parenting decision you make, or feel guilty about a particular part of your parenting identity, you can easily detach from yourself. That causes you to rely on others' ideas, on parenting strategies that don't fit with your unique perspective on life, and lead you to make decisions that you can't even explain for yourself. The rupture that shame creates has to be repaired if you are going to be able to effectively reflect, heal, and grow from that decision you made. If you don't reconnect with yourself, the whole shame-proofing of your parenting idea goes up in smoke. When parents feel detached from a piece of their parenting identity, they develop and use parenting defense mechanisms. These parenting defense mechanisms make it difficult to repair a rupture—even in yourself. I have worked with so many parents whose confidence has been shattered from this level of detachment that they no longer trust their judgment and no longer believe they can make healthy choices for their family.

Peace is not the absence of conflict, but the ability to cope with it.

—*Mahatma Ghandi*

This truth is why shaming parents is so detrimental to families. Shame physically and emotionally hurts. When parents shame their children, it hurts. When people shame parents, it hurts. No one can repair a piece of their identity or make a better decision in the future when they are stuck in the pain of the rupture that division caused. It's not about making a parent aware of the mistakes they made or the decision you don't agree with; it becomes about helping the parent reconcile that decision or that mistake with their growth as a parent, so they can reflect and grow from it, as opposed to detaching and burying it to manage the pain.

Can you see in the rupture and repair cycle how important it is for you to shame-proof your parenting? It is integral to getting into a space of empathy and reflection, in order to repair the ruptures that occur in your family, whether it be one that you're coping with yourself or one that occurred between you and your child.

If you're still with me, and you agree with this concept, then I guess you're wondering, *How do you repair a rupture?*

Siegel and Hartzell posited a few techniques, such as centering yourself and reflecting upon the situation.[13] But under the concept of shame-proofing your parenting, I have a few more techniques to add:

---

13   Hartzell, M. & Siegel, D. Parenting from the inside out: How a deeper self-understanding can help you raise children who thrive (1st ed.), 2005 New York: J.P. Tarcher/Penguin.

Use family meetings to get everyone involved in supporting and repairing the rupture. When you can all look at what's happened and come up with a solution together, it strengthens your bond with each other, it helps everyone learn more about each other, and it helps take the pressure off you as the parent to have all the answers. Too many times in repair, you think you have to do it all alone, but having others' perspectives helps get to a solution that resonates for everyone in your family. It also allows you to be more aware of how your family looks at the situation, and keeps you aware of your humanness and your own biases in repairing ruptures.

Be honest. We just talked about honesty being the best policy. In repairing ruptures, diplomacy and the desire to shield your child from your humanness is not helpful. When you, or your child, make mistakes, and you own up to it, you give your child permission to be just as human too. You show your child what it looks like to let your emotions get the best of you and equally what it looks like to move through that emotion to finding a healthy solution. This is invaluable in shame-proofing your parenting: it helps you realize that you are raising an imperfect human while being an imperfect human yourself. In my opinion, that's the crux of what a shame-proof parent strives to accomplish.

Society's influence and your reactions

No matter how much you try to keep out the outside world, we are inevitably pulled in the moment we take on our parenting identity. Some of this is due to the current way we see parents. The world sees children as an extension of a parent, as opposed to a separate human with their own life journey. We force parents to be accountable for their children, while simultaneously taking away their faculty of intuition with constant shaming and shifts in parenting social consciousness. It's a conundrum that you are dealing with as you read this book—hell, it's probably why you picked up this book.

But until we change the pressure we place on parents, your shame-proof parenting is going to be your best shield when society's ever-shifting ideals bombard you and your parenting.

One thing I constantly hear from parents in terms of society's influence on their parenting identity relates to putting kids in social situations. The common theme is: "I know my kid does bad with social situations, but I'm taking him to this XYZ event because he's got to learn how to be 'normal' and social." Have you ever had that thought? Or, maybe it's more about you wanting and desperately needing to be around other humans and you're tired of your child stopping you from doing that?

These pressures are so common—and normal because of our societal perception of what it means to be human. The common ideology is that you should know how to manage your feelings, behaviors, and thoughts at all times, and anyone who doesn't know how to do this is abnormal. This is a tough spot to be in as you vacillate between connecting with your child, trusting your intuition, knowing who your child is, and wanting your child to be able to function in society.

Parents of special needs kids feel this pressure of shame acutely.

> What turned out to be a typical errand at the post office disturbed me to my core. My son wasn't harming anyone. Sometimes waiting in long lines can be overwhelming for him and we were in a really long line. He gets sensory issues when too many people are around. It can make him nervous. A man told me that my child was bad and would grow up to be a disrespectful thug. I explained to him my child was Autistic and he told me no wonder I couldn't control him and that I should have kept him contained at home. I told him I am not ashamed of my child and he is a person, not an animal and this is America...I don't have to leave him anywhere. Another woman in the line agreed with him and told me that my child was bad because I was a bad mother.

I had to tell them both, Autism is a disability—not a behavior issue. It is something that cannot be changed or corrected, but should be understood. One in 88 children have Autism, and every second, each child's life changes with that diagnosis. EVERYONE heard me stating statistics and facts in that government building. Parent shaming needs to end.

This mom shared this story with me as a post that she shared on social media. She stated that she shared it because she had been following my end parent shaming campaign and felt that she could stand up for her child when someone shamed her for not knowing how to control her child.

Whether your child is introverted, on the autism spectrum, strong-willed, shy, or something else, her identity is not going to change (just like yours hasn't). That doesn't mean we cannot learn coping skills to navigate in the world. It just means that who we are, and the acceptance of our loved ones for who we are, is integral to our self-worth and self-esteem. So, if you are constantly being asked to go against your identity to be socially "normal," you're essentially chipping away at your identity. And as we learned in the section above, that creates disconnect and detachment, leading to making decisions that don't feel right to us, and creating more shame. That's the shame cycle working against you; it's the cycle that you will be able to identify and deal with when you adopt the shame-proof parenting paradigm.

Now imagine that same cycle for your child, but add in the fact that they don't have the option to not participate because you—their parent— is forcing them to participate in a social activity that doesn't feel right for them. Can you see why behaviors arise and conflict prevails in your family?

As you shame-proof your parenting and yourself, you get better at standing your ground for what you know is best for your family. You're not deterred by what you "should be doing;" rather, you are obsessed with what you know is best for you. This trickles down to your child and your family. You stop trying to force them into society's ideals about what they should do, and you focus on their strengths and understand their weaknesses so you don't chip away at their identities.

All the self-help books talk about this brand of self-acceptance. And in the shame-proof parenting framework, it becomes a great model for how to be authentically human for your child.

Respect falls under the umbrella of self-acceptance. For some reason when it comes to parenting and raising kids, respect has become synonymous with absolute compliance. We have a difficult time listening to parents who say XYZ is what's best for my family—calling them weird, abnormal, and shaming them. And we do the same thing to children who we have labeled as "strong-willed," because we no longer have the capacity for endure different perspectives without conflict. This issue pressures parents to force their child to meet expectations that the child cannot adhere to, and illustrates behavior to rebel against. This turns into shame and disrespect, when really it's just you and your family desperately asking to be seen as you are, rather than what others think you should be.

I see this mostly in families that go against the grain, like attachment parents or homeschooling parents or vegan parents. We see parents who adopt these styles of parenting as "trying too hard" and wonder "why can't they just be normal?" When I work with parents who identify in these camps, what I hear time and time again is that no one gives them a space to share why they chose these styles of parenting. All they get is judgment and assumptions about their parenting. This can be even harder when your child is having to shoulder the burden of this from adults who try to pigeonhole them into labels, because your child does not adhere to social norms. The idea here is, that while there are social norms that many of us adhere to and live in without much fanfare, there are going to be families that live outside of those norms for reasons that are unique to their life experiences. In my opinion, as long as no one is being harmed, then they have a right to do this.

In this concept, there is no clear set of rules to guide you. The route to getting through is what we have been talking about this whole book—you've got to get to know yourself and your family. There is no short cut. And the good news is that you get plenty of opportunities to do this. It doesn't have to be as formal as a family meeting. Every day, you and your child are experiencing life together. Ask about it; talk about it; stop trying to make everything a life lesson/Saturday morning special. It's those small moments together that help you bypass society's influence on you. It's those small moments that lead up to bigger moments. When you only notice the negative moments, the not so good moments, of course you lead up to more conflict. But both positive, small moments and bigger moments of conflict are a part of your life together as a family—and your identity as a parent. Shame-proofing your parenting is understanding this truth.

Being able to stand up for YOU

As I stated in the above section, I love the parents who tend to go against the grain in how they raise their children and develop their parenting identity (i.e., attachment parents, vegan parents, crunchy parents, etc.). I love these parents, because the very nature of how they choose their parenting decisions creates a space for them to stand up for their family. In other words, choosing to adopt practices that aren't the norm, sets the stage for families to stand up for what they truly believe in. However, sometimes I notice that parents who have not adopted more uncommon parenting styles feel less inclined to speak up for themselves—they seem to feel that because they're not part of a parenting style that has a name or a following, then they should just blend into the background and do what everyone else is doing. For instance, I've never heard a parent back down when their child has a peanut allergy, or give in to activities when it disagrees with their religious beliefs. But if their child is acting out and it makes others uncomfortable (whether because of a diagnosis or not), I see so many parents cower in fear and shame.

If you are willing to look at another person's behavior towards you as a reflection of the state of their relationship with themselves rather than a statement about your value as a person then you will over a period of time cease to react at all.

—Yogi Bhajan

Being able to stand firm when you're choosing connection over discipline, or when you're making a decision about your child's health, is integral to shame-proofing your parenting. And, let me be clear, this is not me standing on a controversial soapbox. I will not tell you to not vaccinate or to spank your child. What I will do however is give you space to think about why you have chosen these ideas in your parenting.

In shame-proof parenting, this is about minimizing the shame you feel for your decisions, by being informed and knowing your options. No parenting decision is made lightly, no matter how impulsive or uninformed others might think it was. I have seen parents lament and stew on everything from spoiling their child materially, to deciding on medical treatment that they are unsure of. Each of these decisions is gut wrenching for a parent, because none of us can foresee the future. Each parent is hoping that the decision they make right now is going to be beneficial to their child in the future. When we shame parents for those decisions, instead of listening to the story and their path to this decision, we stifle their decision-making process and create parents who no longer know how to stand up for themselves. This creates a path that models for their children, that believing in yourself is only viable when it's with the acceptance of others. Parents under this pressure often continuously make decisions that undermine their sanity and disconnect themselves from their children. When parents are stripped of the space to stand up for themselves, they resort to isolation (a common parenting defense mechanism) and making decisions that may or may not be the most informed, or the best for them and their families in the long run.

The shame-proof parenting framework gives you that space. It says make this decision, fail or succeed with it, and take time to reflect on how that affects your parenting identity and your family's overall health. It says stop allowing others to say yay or nay, and rather take their ideas as suggestions that you bring back to your family to find the solution that works for you.

I am a huge proponent of getting the information that you need to make the most informed decision for your family, constantly assessing if that decision is still viable, and seeking support to make shifts when needed. I encourage my parents to realize that there are always two sides to any decision, and no side is all con or all pro. When we give parents the space to weigh both sides—without judgment or shame—we give parents the power to make healthy decisions for their families. This is another pillar of shame-proof parenting. When you commit to this framework, you don't stop when you make a mistake or get the wrong information. You go inward, into your family and you say, "Okay, what's next?" That is how you get more empowered and confident.

Your kids can develop their own identity

This is something that I talk about a lot: Your identity is yours, and that is also true for your children.

Of course, when your kids are young, you are going to show them how to navigate life and master basic human functions. A concept came up during a parenting workshop I facilitated: the idea of first-generation families, or second-generation families, where the parents were talking about culture, religion, or spirituality. The parents bring their children to this country from their home country, and then the kids are raised in American culture. A common issue that I run into when I work with children from second and on generations is this: they are raised without all of the influence of their parents' culture, religion, or spirituality, so how does that multicultural influence affect the parent-child relationship? I'll get into how culture influences your shame-proof parenting in another chapter, but for now let's talk about how to leave space for your child to have her own identity, while still keeping your parenting shame-proof.

When you raise your child, you bring with you all the generational and cultural influence that makes you who you are. You're very aware of it all because you were raised in it; however, your kid was raised in American culture and they are going to be more influenced by the culture in which they were born and raised. In short, they don't have the same influences you had.

This cultural difference will make your child different from you. And one of the key pieces of shame-proofing your parenting is realizing that each member of your family is an individual human. That can be difficult to deal with as you watch your child make mistakes or choices you disagree with, and you—with your years of experience over your child—can see the trajectory of what their decisions will look like. Even more so, since we live in a world where you are judged by how your children fare in life, you have a lot invested in how the humans under your care make decisions. But this truth is exactly why it's so important to shame-proof your parenting. If your identity is wrapped up in your child, there is no way that child can forge his own identity. He will forever be tied to you and what you think is best. She will not have any space to create her own identity out of successes and failures the way you did.

That's where the conundrum of this whole parenting thing rears its head. As you read this book, you have probably realized that you have broken away from what your parents wanted and dreamed for you, and instead you became the person you are now. There is definitely room for debate about whether you like the person you have become, but this is who you are, nonetheless. You have survived the worst hardships and have celebrated the most amazing successes—all while forging an identity separate from what your parents originally envisioned for you. And now, you are on the cusp of doing the same for your child.

Every human starts out as a vision for their parents and eventually grows into their own unique human. This is the foundation of shame-proof parenting: not to solely use your child as your main source of identity and validation, but to raise a human with his own identity, as a result of being nurtured by you. I know, it's a crazy cycle. But it's one that we as humans must undergo to continue this species—and the more healthily we go about doing it, the more healthy and thriving our human race becomes.

Act as if what you do makes a difference. It does.

—William James

Allowing your child to have her own identity is definitely a huge struggle for you as a parent. But in shame-proofing your parenting, it is imperative that you leave space for your child to define her own identities, so you aren't able to take all the credit for her successes AND all the shame for her failures. Rather, you can support and bolster your child as she traverses through life, no matter how she does that, in a way that helps her develop a healthy sense of self.

I worked with a family where Dad worked in law enforcement and had come to believe that most of the world was a dangerous place. He knew that his view of the world was skewed because of his job, but that did not stop him from projecting those fears on his two children, who were now teens and looking for more autonomy. The images he would conjure up in sessions about his children being kidnapped, harmed, or entangled in illegal activities would make his kids laugh and dismiss him. That dismissal gave him the clout to call them immature, and his insults about their maturity prevented his kids from seeing the validity behind his worries. During one session, all I did was point this out to them— that Dad was basically creating an identity for his children that made them immature kids who wouldn't be able to discern danger in their environment without his involvement. That revelation in session, paired with space for both the kids and the dad to talk about their real fears and anxieties, was enough to help Dad loosen his grip on them and set limits that allowed the teens a chance to show that they could make decisions, even if there were mistakes, and learn from them with Dad's help. This dad learned that he had to let his children make decisions on their own, so they all could see what kind of humans they were growing into. Was it easy for this dad? No. Did he let go of his grip without making mistakes himself? Not at all. But what we figured out in our work together is that identity is forged in mistakes and in support for learning from those mistakes.

Although allowing your child to be his own person will test your sanity and your strength, in the long term it allows you to be a support for him, as opposed to being shamed because you didn't educate him the way someone else thinks you should have.

Conclusion

Every parent I know is affected by their environment. All the to-dos, shuffling from here to there, and pressures of trying to do this parenting thing right all weigh on your shoulders. But the same thing occurs for your child. Children go through the pressures of trying to maintain their grades, manage social interactions, and master their autonomy, all while trying to fit into the expectations you have for them, some of which are more about what others think about your family as opposed to who your children really are. The shame-proof framework will not stop these instances from testing you or your children. What it will do is teach you that being shame-proof gives you a stable foundation for managing and navigating these tough times. I like to say that being shame-proof will give you a problem-solving perspective on life and parenting, as opposed to a catastrophizing lens that often leads us to hide and disconnect. But what happens when there are immediate behavior issues—like, say, your child is having a physical altercation with another person's child? That's where having your shame-proof emergency kit comes in handy.

THE SHAME-PROOF PARENTING EMERGENCY KIT

Learn to sit with not knowing the answers. It creates the space for wisdom and insight to unfold.

—Cheryl Richardson

All this talk about who you are, your identity, your child's identity, and what it truly means to be a shame-proof parent is all great and good, but what about when your child is refusing to get in the car for practice, or is hitting her younger sibling, or is being a complete asshole.

The good news is that shame-proof parenting is not all about theory and introspection. There are also practical tools you can use for emergencies. So, what does your shame-proof parenting emergency kit consist of? Let's find out.

A lot of my clients and parents during workshops want to know the answer to one big question: how do you control a child's behavior? And while many know we are not really going to control our child's behavior, what they are referring to is how do you manage a behavior issue when it presents itself. For example, your toddler is biting, your child is being disrespectful, or your teenager is refusing to come home before the curfew. These are deep behavioral problems, and as a parent you are thinking, "I have to rein this kid in so that it doesn't continue into a behavior other people think is acceptable" (or some variation on this sentiment). The question then becomes: what do you do in that moment?

You are watching your child behave just completely wrong. His behavior is either hurting himself or someone else. And you don't have time for a sit-down chat or family meeting. What's the emergency behavior kit for remaining shame-proof?

The interesting thing is that when we actually pull back the layers on any behavior, you can bet that ten times out of ten, it's a response to a need not being met. Who should meet that need and when it should be met is always up for debate. But the idea is that your child has reached the limit of their understanding and available resources, so he is resulting to a primitive way of achieving his need.

This is how we *all* experience our needs. What separates us is not maturity but whether we have the tools to be aware of what we need and to express that need in a healthy way. And then we still need the tools to be patient while someone helps us meet that need. Having a need met in a way that is healthy and actually accomplishes the goal we set out, is a process that we will explore in this chapter.

The delayed gratification skill

When I took a course on nonviolent parenting, which is a paradigm shift in our perspective about parenting based on the work of Marshall B. Rosenberg's nonviolent communication, I learned what it really means to uncover the needs behind a behavior. Ruth Beaglehole, the creator of the nonviolent parenting curriculum, explained to me once during a training class session that needs are never in conflict, but the ways that we attempt to meets those needs are where the issues arise. This statement couldn't be more true.

> *We either make ourselves miserable, or we make ourselves strong. The amount of work is the same.*
>
> —Carlos Castaneda

We all have needs, and we all want those needs to be met. But we also need to learn how to achieve that and how to manage the time between having the need and having the need met. That space between recognizing that we have a need and when the need actually gets met is called delayed gratification. The idea of delayed gratification is one that usually gets tied to rewards and waiting to receive a reward. However, for this discussion on creating your shame-proof parenting emergency kit, I would like to make it a skill that is necessary for having our needs met. Essentially, when we lack this delayed gratification skill, we have a terrible time waiting for our "reward"—in this case our needs to be met.

Remember the needs inventory checklist? This checklist details known and not so well known needs that we all have, or that we could all have at any given time. (see the Shame-Proof Parenting Needs Inventory figure on page 153). Let's take the need of *belonging*, which falls under the *connection* banner of our needs inventory. This is a need we often seek out in unhealthy ways, and if we don't know how to ask for that feeling of belonging, it's going to be difficult to help a child figure out how to fulfill that need herself.

Oftentimes, belonging looks like wanting to feel close to someone. A lot of times I have seen both children and parents use forceful behaviors, like demanding time be spent with them, to have that need met. And if you're feeling lonely or expect another person to make you feel like you belong, you can go about getting that by yelling, threatening, being physically aggressive, or even attempting to intimidate. It can be hard to sit with feelings of not belonging or feeling left out. However, when we learn to have these uncomfortable feelings, we can stand in them a bit longer while we find the words or behaviors that can achieve those needs. That's where delayed gratification comes into play.

So how do we build up our delayed gratification muscles so that we can withstand uncomfortable feelings long enough to find solutions to expressing our needs, and getting them met without causing a war in our home?

Studies[14] have found that the best way to learn the skill of delayed gratification is to have many predictable experiences in our lives, as opposed to having too many unpredictable experiences.

That sounds vague, I know. And it goes against the idea of what it means to live life. Being able to roll with unpredictable experiences is what builds resilience and helps you to not freak out when things don't go your way. And you'd be right. But when it comes to learning delayed gratification, being able to predict when something is going to happen trains your child's brain to expect that things will happen when you say they will. This is not too difficult to maneuver when you think about it.

The key is to start with small gestures that allow you and your child to see that things will occur as expected, without leaving the safety of your relationship. For example, we've talked about holding family meetings and keeping them set at the same day and time each week. When you do this, and your child comes to expect that there will be a space given to air her issues freely each week, it'll be easier to remind her that she has a space to talk about her issues, as opposed to lashing out during the week because she feels like no one is hearing her.

This brings us back to the need for belonging. When you and your child know that there will be this space to feel included in what's going on with the family, the likelihood that someone feels left out will decrease, especially when this need is given a name so everyone can acknowledge that it is not abnormal to want to feel like they belong. (A great way to do this is to validate that it's okay to want to feel connected to each other, as opposed to telling the person having this need that he is clingy or needy.) The instances of acting out to be heard will most likely decrease too. This happens because you and your child begin to expect that there will be space to be heard and feel included, as opposed to never knowing if or when this need will be acknowledged.

---

14   Clear, J. 40 Years of Stanford Research Found That People With This One Quality Are More Likely to Succeed. JamesClear.com, 2017. Retrieved 7 November 2016, from http://jamesclear.com/delayed-gratification

In the work that I do, I think both parents and kids can develop more patience with each other and develop a delayed gratification practice that allows each person to be heard and each person's needs to be met. We live in such a fast-paced world that slowing down to hear one another is a constant struggle, but you'll learn in this chapter that this is exactly what we have to learn to do to resolve conflict and change behavior.

> *People have said, "Don't cry" to other people for years and years, and all it's ever meant is, "I'm too uncomfortable when you show your feelings. Don't cry." I'd rather have them say, "Go ahead and cry. I'm here to be with you."*
>
> *—Fred Rogers*

What to do when my kid displays unwanted behaviors?

I am happy that this book is really focusing on the human aspect of parenting, and not simply the role of the parent. I truly believe that it's the understanding that everyone has human moments when our emotions overwhelm us, and our logical set of coping skills cannot stop these emotions all the time. In those human moments of your child's behavior, it can like an affront to who you are and what you stand for as a parent. It's easy to forget that your child is having a reaction to the situation at hand, just as all humans do. It's not a calculated plan to undermine your parenting, but rather a human reaction to attempting to get your needs met. A child's behavior looks a lot different than the ones we display as adults. But when children have that "I am overwhelmed with emotion" moment—an "I am overwhelmed with what's going on in my life" experience—they think, "I am going to do X, Y, or Z to get my need met."

The same thing happens with us as adults. Our not-so-nice behaviors are indicators that we are overwhelmed. You yell; you shut down; you don't talk; you punish. You do whatever you think is best to make your voice heard and to get your needs met.

Shame-Proof Parenting
NEEDS INVENTORY CHECKLIST

This checklist can be used to develop the skill of identifying needs, especially as it pertains to some of the more uncommon needs that humans can express.

Autonomy

- [ ] Choice
- [ ] Freedom
- [ ] Space
- [ ] Spontaneity

Integrity

- [ ] Honesty
- [ ] Authenticity
- [ ] Presence
- [ ] Empathy
- [ ] Equality
- [ ] Understanding

Spirituality

- [ ] Hope
- [ ] Awareness
- [ ] Discovery
- [ ] Understanding
- [ ] Order
- [ ] Peace
- [ ] Inspiration
- [ ] Stimulation
- [ ] Purpose

Physical Connection

- [ ] Air
- [ ] Food
- [ ] Rest/Sleep
- [ ] Sexual expression
- [ ] Shelter
- [ ] Safety
- [ ] Water
- [ ] Touch
- [ ] Movement

Interdependence
(aka Connection)

- [ ] Communication
- [ ] Belonging
- [ ] Acceptance
- [ ] Community
- [ ] Support
- [ ] Trust
- [ ] Consistency
- [ ] Respect/Self-respect
- [ ] Inclusion
- [ ] Safety
- [ ] Warmth
- [ ] Nurturing

Life and Meaning

- [ ] Celebration of life
- [ ] Creativity
- [ ] Mourning
- [ ] Grief
- [ ] Beauty
- [ ] Purpose
- [ ] Discovery
- [ ] Harmony
- [ ] Inspiration
- [ ] Contribution
- [ ] Discovery
- [ ] Learning
- [ ] Participation
- [ ] Challenge
- [ ] Self-expression

Fun & Relaxation

- [ ] Joy
- [ ] Humor
- [ ] Laughter
- [ ] Silliness
- [ ] Outside activities
- [ ] Indoor activities
- [ ] Movement
- [ ] Mindfulness

References:
Adapted from Rosenberg, M. B. (2003). Nonviolent communication: a language of life. Encinitas, CA: PuddleDancer Press.
Adapted from Bengiohole, R. & Goldberg, S.B. (2011). Nonviolent parenting teacher training (Curriculum). Los Angeles, CA.

Still, this discussion on delayed gratification and acknowledging that kids are just like us when it comes to expressing our emotions through our behaviors, does not answer the question I posed at the beginning of the chapter: what do I do when my kid displays unwanted behaviors? The good news is that you do have a few options to manage these behaviors when they arise:

Make sure that your child and others around are safe. Always ask yourself: is my child, and are others around my child, safe? If the answer is yes, then you have opened up another line of strategies to use. If the answer is no, then you have to help your child to safety. For younger kids, it's simply getting them to another area away from the situation that is triggering them, or getting others away from the situation if your child is refusing to leave. You can let your child know what you are doing by using a phrase like, "Wow this looks really unsafe; I am going to help you; Mom is going to help you right now; Daddy is going to help you right now." This lets your child know what is happening and might even pull them out of their immediate tantrum. It doesn't mean that the conflict is resolved, it just means that you are moving them to a space where they can calm down and where you can start to find the solutions for the issue.

Deescalate the tension. For older kids who cannot be taken away physically, as in you cannot pick them up and take them somewhere else, you can either ask them to move away from what's triggering them (remember this is not a punishment but a chance to deescalate the tension by letting them go where they need to calm down), or you can ask others to move into another area to calm down. If there is too much room for physical harm, seek the help of local law enforcement. That might seem like a huge deal, but it's better than allowing yourself or others to get hurt if your older child is refusing to calm down and is threatening harm to self or others. If you are able to deescalate the situation, let your older child know where you will be if they want to talk when they are calmed down. This might happen in the same day the outburst occurred, or it could happen later. The idea is to deescalate first, problem solve second—especially with an older child.

Hear your child out. Remember that most behavior is an attempt to get needs met or feelings heard. Very rarely is your child trying to hurt you for the sake of hurting you. If they are, this is a deeper issue that I will talk about at the end of the chapter. To make sure that your child will actually talk so that you can hear them, you also need to create a safe space for them to dump all their issues. When we feel unsafe, we are in a part of our brain called the "reptilian brain," which houses the flight or fight responses.[15] Think about that for a minute: if we are in a flight or fight part of our brain, do you think we will be able to have a real conversation about our feelings?

In fact, our feelings reside in a higher part of our brain that cannot be accessed until our flight or fight response is turned off. This means that when our children feel unsafe for whatever reason, they are unable to have real conversations about what is going on for them, because they are thinking about defending themselves and do not have access to their feelings. For almost every outburst situation though, once the kid has calmed down and feels safe to talk about it, you've got to make sure that you figure out what was going on.

And you can do that in several ways:

1. Don't judge: The biggest barrier to talking to you is the fear that you will judge them for what they think or feel. Let your child know that you are open to hearing what they think before making any comments.

2. Ask before giving advice: After you've let your child talk, you can simply ask if they want advice or if they just want a space to rant.

---

15   Bryson, T. & Siegel, D. The whole-brain child: 12 revolutionary strategies to nurture your child's developing mind., 2011. New York: Delacorte Press.

3. Don't overreact: Some things that your child chooses to share with you will be intense—a friend's mental health, their own sadness and disappointment, being offered substances with friends, or even having dating issues. If you need time to process, you can say, "That's a really intense issue, and I thank you for sharing it with me. Do you mind if I take a minute to gather my thoughts, and I can talk to you about it [set a time to come back to it]?"

4. Stick with them: There will be times when your child will be experiencing something that seems trivial or unimportant to you. Or, there will be times that your child is not able to express what they are feeling in a healthy way. In both cases, you can be triggered to dismiss what's going on as a kid issue and jump to lecturing. I challenge you to do this instead: Tell them, "I am here to talk when you are ready. I'm sorry that I do not understand what is going on for you, but I would like to. So, come talk to me when you're ready and I will listen without judgment."

Words matter. Choose carefully the words you speak to your children, to others, to yourself. Words have a way of becoming truths that we believe about ourselves.

—*L.R. Knost*

Do your own reflection. You may be able to take what you know about your kid, and you can probably diagnose pretty well what happened. For example, if you have siblings that are constantly fighting over the same toys, then you pretty much know this toy sparked their current conflict. Instead of being exasperated about similar conflicts arising in your children and wishing they'd just learn to work it out, be their mirror. First, take some time to reflect on what may be causing the constant conflict, think of one or two things that could be the underlying cause, and share them with your children. Then back out and see if they can problem solve the issue themselves. Even if they can't, you are giving space for reflection and problem solving to emerge as a way to manage the behavior, as opposed to you letting the frustration get in the way and solving the issue for them.

It's the same thing with your older kids. If you know that your kid is someone kind of rebellious, you have to be honest with yourself. Reflect on what this rebellion triggers in you, and reframe rebellion as your child being an independent thinker. This doesn't dismiss their behaviors or sugarcoat them, but it allows you to open up a space for curiosity instead of discipline and punishment. Before you start the discussion—and before you lunge into an argument over your child's behavior—you've got to do that reflection about how they trigger you. Again, your reflection will change the direction of the discussion, not stop it from happening. It will allow you to model what it looks like to manage emotions even when you disagree, and gives your children more space to explain themselves instead of your biases taking up the majority of the room in the discussion.

Share your reflection with your child in an honest conversation. After you've done that reflection, go to the kid and share with them the reflections you had.

For the younger kids, you're teaching them more about themselves. For example, you can share that you noticed that they are always arguing about the same toy, and that they do have some valid points and that things sometimes seem unfair, but that the last three times the conflict has got so bad you've had to separate them. Essentially, you are exploring their feelings of not being treated fairly. As you listen to your child or share with them that you have heard all this, you develop empathy for him. You think, "No wonder he's so adamant about getting that toy back, he knows I'm going to side with his sister because she's younger." Then, try working on some solutions for what your child can do when he is feeling this unfairness. Maybe you both can decide that if he says, "Mom you're being unfair," that this be your signal for thinking of another way to help the siblings resolve the toy issue. In this, we move back into strengthening our delayed gratification skill. Your child begins to trust that you will hear his feelings and can give you more space to help him resolve this issue with his sibling.

This looks a bit different with older kids because they require a bit more autonomy to find solutions to their issues, and that often clashes with your own level of patience and delayed gratification skills. I caution parents that older kids tend to push your buttons more than younger kids, because they are developing the logical/reasoning parts of their brains and are no longer solely focused on themselves but also on the injustices they perceive in their world. When you talk to your older children, I encourage that you stay away from lecturing, preaching, questioning, and advising, because these actions tend to trigger complaining, refusing, lying, and begging. Instead, you can try these tools to shift the focus to coming to a solution together:

1. Give each other space: I highly encourage this tool when you are really upset with your child, and when you can see that your child is really upset with you. Giving each other space, which might include walking away for a short amount of time, allows you both time to think about what happened and calm down. Then, you can come back together to find a solution—or you might both decide it's not worth discussing anymore. The idea here is that you both agree that you're both too upset to problem solve and that you will come back to it in X amount of time. When you come back together to discuss it, make sure you're both cooler about the issue. Here's the caveat: if when you come back to it you both get upset again, give more space. It's not about rushing to the finish line to resolve the issue. It's about coming to a solution that makes you both feel heard.

2. Don't take it personal: It's so difficult not to take it personal when we push each other's buttons. But the reason we get under each other's skin, is we have unmet needs and are not able to access the more acceptable ways to obtain them. Taking it personal will only heighten the offense and make it harder to reach a resolution. The best way to not take it personal is to remind yourself that you and your child are both trying to have your needs met. You can either get curious about what need they are trying to fulfill, get quiet to reflect about your own needs, or do a combination of both. The idea is that you're not making a rash judgment that will lead you to react to an imagined slight from your child.

3. Get to know each other: This one is integral to knowing what triggers each other. Parents sometimes forget that they can trigger their children just as their children trigger them. To get a good grip on this tool, observe your child during calm times and watch what really makes them upset. Also, help your child learn more about yourself by telling them what things make you upset or irritable. This one can be done whenever or wherever you and your child are. It just requires you both to slow down enough to recognize each other's personality and nuances. It might be a good idea to have one-on-one time with your child so you can have uninterrupted time to learn about each other.

There is no guarantee you can control anyone's behavior

Any altercation or behavior between you and your child will always be an external sign to some internal struggle that is going on. So, even though I'm calling this an emergency kit, there is no guarantee you can control your child's behavior, your spouse's, or anyone else's.

I know, I know! When your child is acting out, you feel like you need a quick way to get the kid to just do what you want her to do. But, here's the deal: it's going to be difficult to use any parenting strategy when you and your child are experiencing negative emotions. If you're frustrated because of their behavior and they are feeling very strongly and displaying negative behavior, there are few healthy parenting strategies that will quell the behavior. Anything outside of making sure you, your child, and everyone around is safe, and getting your child away from the triggering stimuli, will most likely make the behavior worse.

So, the long of it is this: you have to do the work before having the space and energy needed to manage the situation when it occurs.

But I can see you saying: there has to be a set of strategies to stop a meltdown, or stop a tantrum, or stop your older kid from being an asshole! And, you're right, there are! But let's look at another scenario:

Taking care of your car is time-consuming sometimes, especially if you have an older car. You have to do regular oil changes, keep the gas tank full, and do occasional maintenance based on how many miles you've done. All this makes sense right? Well, what if you skipped an oil change (for whatever reason: you forgot, you were in a financial lull, you didn't want to take it in, etc.). Would filling up the tank regularly take the place of getting that oil change? Okay, let's go a bit deeper. What if the engine light came on and you checked your vehicle manual (let's pretend you responsibly kept it in the glove compartment to check when you need to know what maintenance is due on the car) to see that the scheduled maintenance is to rotate the tires, check fluids, and get maintenance on the transmission? But, of course, you've got a million things to do and you can't have your car in the shop, or wait for hours at the shop, while the car is serviced, so you just pop into a Jiffy Lube for a quick oil change—oh, and you keep putting gas in the car regularly. What do you think is going to happen to the car over time if you keep putting off the scheduled maintenance? Yep, you're right! It's most likely going to fall apart on you or give you more trouble than taking it in for service would have been.

Even when you put a spare tire on your car because of a flat tire, while that might be the emergency strategy, you eventually have to take it in to get a new tire because no one can drive on a spare for long periods of time.

But that's what we do when we ignore the process of getting to the bottom of a behavior in our child. When you manage it quickly with an emergency parenting strategy, you're essentially driving on a spare and putting gas in the tank, when you need an oil change and a new set of tires. You're prolonging the behavior by ignoring it, and allowing it to escalate until it becomes frustratingly unmanageable.

That's why the emergency kit is just for that—emergencies. As soon as the emergency is over, you need to get back to the work of shame-proofing your parenting.

The secret to change is to focus all of your energy not fighting the old, but on building the new.

—Socrates

A need that goes ignored triggers an unhealthy defense mechanism

Before you beat yourself up for doing this, we all do it in all our relationships, because conflict is messy and we'd rather avoid it; let's be realistic about that. We've established that all behaviors are actions that we use to achieve our needs. (Have I beat that horse to death yet?!) Some behaviors are positive and work well to get what we need accomplished. And some, like the ones you're thinking about right now that your child constantly does, disrupt our daily lives. But no matter how we display these behaviors, they all mean the same thing: I have a need, I have a feeling, and this is the best way I know to alert you to it.

The interesting thing is that many of us, including your child, have many ways to show people what we need and how we feel. When these behaviors, sometimes subtle and hard to decipher, are ignored, we all escalate until we are heard, even if that escalation causes more issues for us. For humans, being heard sometimes outweighs the consequences. If you're thinking that you don't do this, think of all the times you've yelled at your kids. Your yelling is an escalation of you calmly asking for a task to be completed, probably multiple times. You've tried everything calmly, you were ignored, and you yelled. Of course, yelling often gets the job done. Everyone scampers away and does the task you asked them to do five times prior, which reinforces that you need to yell to get your voice heard, so you keep doing it. Even if it makes you feel horrible and you feel guilty (or probably more frustrated) that you have to resort to yelling to get anyone to do anything!

Now, that's you! But your children do the same thing. They try to tell you something in a calm way, and if you're saying your child does not have a calm way of telling you something, I'd say get out of your interpretation of calm and start observing what happens in your child before they finally have a meltdown, and I can guarantee that your child does show you in their own calm way that they have a need that you may not notice or that you may ignore. And after not being listened to or heard, they resort to a behavior they know will finally get your attention (yelling, fighting, biting, defiance, disrespect). This behavior, although it comes with consequences, is what they have learned gets them heard. They may get grounded or their stuff taken away, but you've finally stopped what you were doing long enough to hear them. And get this, your child is right. After the discipline and punishment, if you do end up talking about what it is they wanted to talk about, even if it's through nagging and lecturing your child, they see their negative behaviors as a way to be seen.

Now, wouldn't it be nice to be able to bypass some of this to just get to the being heard part? If you said yes, then here's where your shame-proof parenting emergency kit comes into play!

The first piece of it is always to make sure your kid is safe. Once your kid is safe and you've got them away from the problem, they calm down. Great. But you do have to eventually go back to the issue and resolve it. Calming down and/or deescalating the situation is just the first step. If we don't continue to the next steps, then the behaviors will keep happening and might even escalate as the kids get older, because they'll realize no one is going to help them work through this issue. When a child realizes that no one is listening to them or helping with this issue, they feel like they have to get worse to be heard. Your child learns that she's got to not only let go of the idea that she'll ever be heard, but also protect herself from the pain of not being heard to the point where she has so many defenses in place, that trying to get through all of those walls becomes really difficult for a family.

Trust the wait. Embrace the uncertainty. Enjoy the beauty of becoming. When nothing is certain, anything is possible.

—Mandy Hale

By the time your kid gets to be a teen, imagine this metaphorical picture: you have to take your fist and bust through a brick wall each time you attempt to get closer to your kid. After a while, your hands are going to break, you are going to be so bloody that you don't care anymore, or you are going to be in so much pain trying to bust through their wall that you are not going to care anymore. So, you work up the courage to bust through about two of them on your own, then you enlist the help of a professional to get through another two, but that's only four out of the six they have. It gets burdensome, and in my work with families, this is where I see a lot of parents give up. They feel like there is no getting through to their child. Interestingly, that's what it looks like for you and your parenting defense mechanisms. The walls you built up to survive your family of origin are now showing up in how you're reacting to your child and dictating the amount of space you have for your child.

So, it becomes a cycle: you display a behavior to meet a need, it's dealt with in an unhealthy way, you build a wall to defend against this unhealthy encounter, the wall blocks reflection, so you display another behavior to get what you need, this need is also dealt with in an unhealthy way, another wall is created, and so on and so forth.

Here we return to a central theme of this book: "You are a human yourself." By the time you get to be an adult and you make a decision to have a child, how many walls do you think you have built? The defenses that you have developed stem from all the instances where no one helped you navigate those negative encounters, in which you built up walls to protect yourself, and now those negative encounters have become a piece of your human identity, and thus, your parenting identity (think: parenting defense mechanisms).

But as humans, this is how behaviors start. Without reflection, parents will exclaim that they aren't going to be like their parents, or that they know how to control their children so that they don't have to recreate the same parenting they lived through. But we are not dealing with the underlying shame. This is what we all do as humans—put up walls to protect ourselves. Most kids (and adults for that matter) will put up walls so that they don't keep getting punished, they don't keep getting yelled at, or they don't keep getting hurt by the punishment and the yelling. For example, they are still getting yelled at, but the walls they've built provide a barrier to protect them from the pain of their consequences. This apathy that your child develops is usually what a parent is referring to when they exclaim that nothing they do works anymore.

Interestingly enough, it goes into why a lot of parents internalize shame so effectively. You grab ahold of parenting gimmicks so that you don't do to your kids what was done to you, but in doing so, end up ignoring the empathetic, reflective process of what it means to not be like your parents. Then, the shame comes when you display negative reactions to your child's behavior, not because you are a bad parent but just because you have your own stuff. You have your own limits. Essentially, you've got to break through your own walls so that the parenting strategies you choose to use make sense for who you are and who your child is, rather than using those strategies to cover up the messy pieces of being a human and a parent.

So, there is the answer to your question: what do you do when my kid acts up in public, or has a meltdown, or does any other thing that drives you insane as a parent? You do the legwork. It starts with you, and it flows into your relationship with your child. Not to blame you or demonize you, but it starts with who you are, what you've learned, and how this informs the way you raise your child. Reflective parenting can become your emergency parenting kit. In essence, an effective way to manage emergency behaviors is to lean into who you are, what you know about your child, and use that connection as your strategy. Easier said than done, yes. But with practice and patience, it becomes something that you do unconsciously.

There will always be days when there are public meltdowns, there's nothing you can do to control your child's behavior, and you will be shamed by others around you. But you can still control your own reaction, and resist shaming your own children.

I have the privilege of being surrounded by amazing colleagues. Doing this work, it can be lonely, and it can feel daunting. Sometimes I wonder, "Is my message of ending parent shaming even registering?"

Well, I got the answer about a year ago when I met an online colleague in person for a conference we were both attending. After we talked about how good it was to finally meet and how much we felt like we knew each other, my colleague said to me that she had been closely following my #endparentshaming campaign on social media. She said that while she loved it and thought it was time that someone started talking about it, she didn't give much thought to how she was being shamed as a mother until her flight coming to this event. She had decided to make the trip a family vacation as well, so she and her husband brought their two children along (both of whom were under the age of five years old). I knew this colleague to be a very conscious and aware parent, based on the way she discussed and explored her family relationships on social media, and meeting her confirmed that. So, as she relayed her story of being shamed on the airplane, I felt for her.

She explained that both her daughters were used to routines and she knew that while the flight would disrupt their routines, she would be able to manage them because the flight from the east coast to the west coast was not a long one. Well, of course there was a delay and they were stalled at one of the stops along the way. As my colleague tried to manage and empathize with her children's emotions, my colleague talked about how she was feeling as a mom—she was feeling tired, overwhelmed, and frustrated herself because of the delay, but she was also attuned to her children's frustration, fatigue, and anxiety for being out of routine. The prep she had done prior to the trip was not panning out the way she told the children, and they were starting to let her know that they were upset because things were not going as planned. My colleague stated that even through this, she was able to maintain her calm and keep her children calm, so they were able to board their connecting flight without much hassle. However, once they were on the next flight—and because the children's day had been disrupted so—one of her children had a meltdown. The child cried and was inconsolable for a considerable amount of time. The meltdown lasted so long that one of the passengers made a flippant comment about how my colleague needed to learn how to keep control of her child, so that the child would not disturb the rest of the flight. In that moment, my colleague felt a wave of shame and guilt. She felt like she should be able to keep her child under control. She explained that in that moment, she remembered the end parent shaming posts that I had been sharing on social media, and instead of despair or taking out her feelings on her child, my colleague decided to stand up for herself as a parent.

My colleague turned to the passenger and let her know that she was shaming her and that she did not like that. She told the passenger that if they did not have anything positive to contribute, that they please allow her to care for her children the best way she knew how. The passenger did not respond.

After my colleague shared this story, she said that she realized that shame can be so debilitating for parents, and that if she hadn't been connected to me and my message, she most likely would have internalized that shame as being a bad parent rather than standing up for herself and returning to care for her child as her child needed.

When parenting fatigue sets in

Shame-proof parenting is just like sticking to a routine or a diet. Whether it be for physical health or mental well-being, you start off strong. Then, because life gets in the way, you wane a bit. Maybe in the beginning you saw some awesome results, but after a few months you're stagnant in your goals/results, so you get discouraged and you stop.

This can also relate to the strategies you begin to use in your shame-proof parenting emergency kit. You start off talking, being observant, and trying to get to the bottom of what's going on, but you get discouraged because it feels like nothing is changing. But here's the human rub to it all: it's not just that things take time; instead, it's about communication and empathy. When it gets tough to maintain a parenting strategy, be honest about it and look at how you can tweak it, so you and your family don't get so burned out with it. Giving yourself this space to be human—not superhuman, or perfect—actually teaches your children that it's okay to reevaluate things in their world. Not necessarily give up on it, but to reevaluate how it's fitting into their lives. You model that by giving yourself that empathy and communicating why you are reevaluating a decision.

If you want to see a behavior change, if you've gotten to the bottom of what you think is going on, if you have an idea on how to help change it, then talk to your child. Include them in your process so they develop the skill to do the same when they are trying to make changes in their lives. Change cannot happen in isolation. You have to talk about it, even if it's hard. Some conversations will happen once or twice and be done; others may take a few more conversations. Fatigue will set in; frustration will be present. But these feelings are a normal part of the process. Shame-proofing your parenting is more about raising humans who understands the journey of being empathetic with themselves. This means that you have to be a human in this process too, for yourself and for your child.

Stop being afraid of what could go wrong, and start being excited for what could go right.

—*Unknown*

Slow the heck down for heaven's sake

A big struggle for modern parents is the sheer amount of activity our families are involved in. It's easier for self-reflection to happen during the more mundane, quieter times in our lives, but self-reflection doesn't come very easily during a tantrum on the way to soccer practice. Having your child in everything under the sun to help them have a leg up in life actually does the opposite—it teaches them the wrong thing about what it means to be a well-rounded human. Being a well-rounded human does not include a lot of noise and busyness, but rather space for reflection, learning, and growing without judgment. All that stress of running to and fro all the time, for both you as a parent and for your kid, is bound to come out in your relationships.

A lot of the time, we do all this stuff because it means something. There are so many families that believe all the busyness means that they are doing a good job as parents, exposing their children to everything life has to offer. Or, they're giving their child a life they didn't have. Or, any other explanation for why we place so much value on being busy. But I often challenge my parents to be self-reflective and ask themselves: why do I have my child in this activity? Is it because he really wanted it, is it because I really wanted it, or is it a combination of both? This line of questioning will help you assess whether you still need that activity in your lives. This is even more crucial if your child starts pulling with you and fighting you about a particular activity.

This reflection might look something like this:

> *Okay, when we first started it, everyone was excited, you were doing so well; you were winning all the trophies and having so much fun, but now just the mention of it starts a chain reaction in our family. Let's see what's going on here. What is this? Do we still need it? What purpose is it still serving?*

This happens to you sometimes, if you think about it. How many times have you signed up for something that initially was useful, but then somewhere along the line just thinking about participating caused you to shut down. I've noticed that we trudge through things like this and then a year later, we're stuck wondering why we're still doing it. Once you realize that it's no longer serving a purpose in your life, you reassess and decide to either quit it or recommit to it in a more active way. Now, you have to teach your kid to do the same.

One strategy that I empower parents with is to teach your child about grit. As a side effect of knowing your child, you'll get to see whether she has "grit." According to Webster's dictionary, grit is a "firmness of character or [having an] indomitable spirit." In other words, grit means sticking with something even though it's not fun. Grit can be a valuable skill for children to have. When we learn to tough it out, we also learn a lot about ourselves, but what we learn is not always what we thought. Sometimes sticking it out teaches us that we're not cut out for a particular task—

and that's okay! We want to teach our children about the importance of committing to something that will not always be fun to do. Ultimately, that task will help them learn more about who they are and what they're capable of. When you and your child do decide to quit something, make sure there's space to reflect on what worked and didn't work, so that you can turn quitting into a step towards developing more grit in your child.

So, yeah, I know the chapter title was misleading in a sense. You wanted a list of strategies to use to control/discipline/stop your child from displaying unwanted behavior. And you got that! But the heart of effective shame-proof parenting revolves around your relationship with your child and the leg work that you do before the behavior is displayed—legwork that will give you the insight you need to help you and your child work through any issue that arises.

Conclusion

On the whole, a shame-proof parenting emergency kit consists of keeping your child safe and doing the leg work of understanding how your child learns to get their needs met. The idea that you can attend to an unwanted behavior in the moment without truly understanding the underlying motivations, can lead to you and your child building up walls of resistance, creating more disconnection, and exacerbating more intense behaviors to get seen and heard. It's an unhealthy cycle, and one that shame-proof parenting can bring awareness to and, in essence, work to decrease the number of times your family ends up in this cycle. Shame-proof parenting won't take away conflict, but it will teach you how to build a connection instead of a wall. As long as we are connecting to other humans, we will have to manage conflict and behaviors. But with the right perspective on these behaviors, such as understanding that all behavior is an action to get a need met, we are better equipped to work through the issues. Once *you* get that piece, you can help your child get that piece too, so they aren't fighting you so much, thinking that you are plotting against them! It becomes—ta da!—a shame-proofed family that can withstand conflict, maintain connection, and be a safe space to manage life's ups and downs.

There's one more key piece we need to address to truly make this shame-proof parenting philosophy work for you and your family, and that is how to bring in help when you need it. Believe me, if you're going to do this parenting thing as effectively as possible, you're going to need help.

YOU DON'T JUST NEED SUPPORT—YOU NEED A WHOLE SHAME-PROOF VILLAGE

I want to be around people that do things. I don't want to be around people anymore that judge or talk about what people do. I want to be around people who dream, and do things.

—Amy Poehler

I remember working with a mom who had a lot going on in her life. She was raising her younger brother as his kinship caregiver, working for child protective services, and was seven months pregnant with a child of her own. As we worked together to help her manage her family more effectively, she revealed to me that she felt overwhelmed and was second-guessing her decision to get pregnant. As she told me this, I could feel the guilt radiating off of her. She continued that it wasn't that she didn't want to have the child; she just wished that she had more support. As she detailed her daily schedule of seeing kids at her job, making sure her brother had what he needed, and keeping herself healthy for her unborn child, she looked ready to throw in the towel.

When I asked her who she would consider part of her support system, she laughed and said no one. For her, and the life she'd lived, trusting people was not something she was good at doing, and she didn't have many friends or family members that she could call on for support. While she knew that she needed to work on her trust issues, she said that working and being a parent was taking up too much of her time, to actually stop long enough to think about herself at all.

This mother's story echoes the stories I hear from so many parents. They either have difficulty trusting others, or can't find enough people to trust.

And there's no judgment here. The weight and consequence that shame can hold over you makes it damn near impossible to think about yourself, for fear that you are being selfish, or that taking care of yourself takes time away from your child-rearing—which means that you'll raise an asshole. However, this mindset is only one of the ways parents place a barrier on getting help on their parenting journey.

The other barrier is assuming that you are the only one whose child does [insert negative child behavior here], or that everyone else is doing things better than you, or a multitude of other assumptions we hold that stops us from reaching out. Most of these assumptions come from a place of shame that tells you, that if your child is not behaving perfectly, then you must be doing it wrong, and that if someone else's child is performing well, they must be doing it right. It's in these moments that we feel at our worst, we retreat inward, and we build parenting defense mechanisms to protect us from the pain of what others may think about us. It's in this mindset that we isolate, we suffer in anguish, and we feed the self-fulfilling prophecy that we are the only ones struggling in this child-rearing journey.

A dad I was working with sent me this email after reading an article I wrote about parent shaming:

> *I was having a conversation with another parent last week and I wanted to share with you a thought about parent shaming, after reading your great article. Her daughter is struggling right now, and we talked about how as a parent, you know the people who you can be honest about your child's struggle with and who you can't. It's very much OK to brag about your child when someone asks how are they doing, but if they are struggling we don't share that, because we are somehow ashamed... thinking it reflects badly on our parenting. It really is a shame, this feeling of shame. It keeps us from being there for each other as parents, and feels isolating. The truth is, as my friend and I discussed, there are many more teens struggling than sailing through but you would never*

know it, because everyone keeps that to themselves like some dark secret. It's really too bad. I think the thing to do is try to be honest about our children and let go of the thought that somehow everything they are doing (wrong or right) is somehow directly the result of our parenting. By being honest we give others the opportunity to do the same. We'd all be better off, living in the parenting light!!!

This email sheds light on how parenting shame not only changes how we see ourselves and our children, but how it even gets in the way of reaching out to others for support.

With all the time that you've spent reading this book and trying to wrap your head around the shame-proof parenting framework, there is one piece that I purposefully saved for last. It's the one piece that we sometimes forget is valuable, but is really important on our parenting journey. And it's the piece that I feel will really compliment and enhance the shame-proofing that you have already committed to.

It's creating a shame-proof village.

A shame-proof village is more than just camaraderie with other parents. It's more than just getting together to chat and reflect. It becomes a space where you can be truly human and embrace each part of your identity.

The whole point of shame-proofing your parenting is not only to protect and give space to your parenting identity, but also to embrace the fact that you are not solely one role. Your parenting is important. Your role in raising another human is important. But so are all the other pieces of your identity that coalesce to help develop and create your parenting identity.

We've talked about this in parts throughout the book: when you become a parent, all your other experiences and roles inform how you raise your child. There is no way that you forget the life you had before you became a parent for the sake of your child. And there is really no logical reason to even consider doing that. The way we see parents, makes you feel as if the experiences you had prior to having kids pale in comparison to the experiences you'll have while raising kids. This is preposterous, because the lessons you learned before having kids become the foundation for how you help your human learn how to live in the world. Why would forgetting all about that be a benefit for your child?

Your child is a human who will also have multiple roles in their lives. And if you're the model for how all those roles merge into a healthily, imperfect human, then you cannot ignore who you truly are. When you have a shame-proof village, you get to do just that: embrace all the humanness you have with others who are willing and ready to do the same!

So, what is a shame-proof village?

We all know the saying, "It takes a village to raise a child," but what does that really mean? What kind of village are we really talking about?

What if that village is full of people who shame, blame, guilt, and label everything you do as a parent? Would you want to be a part of that village? Would you allow that village to help raise your child? The answer is a resounding no!

So, why do we live in a world where it has become second nature to shame a parent and to label their parenting based on what *we* think is best? We know that children raised in traumatic and stressed homes tend to do worse than children who aren't, but still we bury shame and blame under our superficial mission to save children.

We sometimes forget that having a stressed, guilt-ridden, shamed parent can make a household just as difficult to live in as one that's filled with abuse. That's why it's so important for us to stop letting our "save the child" mindset be the superficial foundation we use to shame parents. This "village" that we currently have is not helpful, nor is it empowering.

And certain parenting gimmicks have unconsciously encouraged us to create smaller, exclusive villages where, unless you believe in that philosophy of parenting, you are excluded. Think of parents who embrace free-range kids or attachment or unschooling. There are some communities ("villages") that have rigid expectations about what kind of parent you'll be within that community. The idea of being an intuitive, eclectic parent who not only embraces the researched parenting strategies, but also learns to lean into the imperfection of being human, is not always welcomed with open arms.

We see exclusive villages play out in everyday life, whether you're trying to adopt a certain parenting style or not. The Mommy and Me groups exclude fathers who can't find public spaces that make them feel like they are valued members of the parenting unit. The luxury Mommy and Me classes make women who don't identify with those bells and whistles feel weird. In the village I grew up with, that close-knit community where people were encouraged to fit in and get along and smile on Sundays, was the same one that caused my mom to try to stuff the reality of our situation away for fear of judgment. In that village, I need you to tell me that I am good; I need the approval of the group in order to survive.

And when these parents remain on the edges of what we call "supportive villages" for parents, where do they get the support that feels good to them?

Again, this is not an attempt to bash the elements of parenting that support and help you. It's opening a space for discussion about what it means to truly create villages that feel authentic and resonate with your uniqueness.

It's time to create a new village that is made strong and enduring by the knowledge that *I am good*. It's about individual self-acceptance. When you know this, you're not looking for the approval of an existing community—especially if that community wants you to change in order to be a part of it. Instead, you go out and make your own village. You create your own tribe based on shared self-love.

Your value doesn't decrease based on someone's inability to see your worth.

—Unknown

That is the message that I am sharing here. When you know who you are, who your family is, and how you work best, you find a peace, a self-acceptance, that allows you to create the village that supports what you need, as opposed to finding a village that tells you who you should be.

In creating a shame-proof village, you get to add support, people, and resources to your village that complement you and your family. That means that it doesn't have to always include other parents who have the same parenting philosophy as you. You can include single friends, painting buddies, yoga classes, and/or Netflix parties.

Many parents believe that no one will understand them unless they have children too—and while that is partly true—it's also true that being around other parents can sometimes be just as suffocating as being around non-parents. The truth is this: when you surround yourself with people who do not support you as you are (no matter which role you're currently in), you don't get what you need to grow, reflect, and make changes that feel right to you.

Thus, creating your shame-proof village actually supports your shame-proof parenting, and helps solidify the notion that being human is not a one-person journey. No one lives in a vacuum. No family does, and no human does. We thrive on the support of surrounding ourselves with people who understand us, whether they share the same roles we live or not. That's the beauty of creating a shame-proof village. You get to find the people who support and love you as an imperfect human, but they don't have to be parents or live the same life experiences that you've had.

Let's create your shame-proof village

Recognize yourself as more than a parent

At the core, shame-proof parenting is about nurturing all aspects of your human identity. You are not just a parent, although it may feel like that's all you are at times. When you create your shame-proof village, you need to also maintain and nurture the aspects of your humanness that help make you feel whole. When you only focus on supporting your parenting identity, and forget the other pieces of your identity that make you whole, you are leaving a huge space for shame and guilt to creep in.

When you identify with only one aspect of yourself, what do you think happens when there are hardships in that area of your identity? You begin to think you're a failure because of the low tide that is this aspect of who you are. When I see parents identify only with who they are as a parent, and only get support for that piece of their identity, I see a lack of confidence and an increase in feelings of inadequacy. This comes from our societal notion that becoming a parent is the greatest thing you will ever accomplish. This unfortunately undermines all the other successes you have had in your life before (and during, and after) you raise your kids, which just perpetuates the idea that once you become a parent, your whole identity should be wrapped up in this role.

Your kids will make you question who you are and what you stand for; that's part of their development. They are developing humans who are taking everything that they're experiencing, trying to reconcile that with what you're teaching them, and creating an identity of their own. When you take this perspective and how much it will fluctuate as your child develops, does it make sense to only validate yourself based on another human's development, successes, and failures?

As much as your child is developing, so are you. You are a human who is still developing and growing. And if you are only nurturing the part of you that is a parent, then the other pieces of your identity are growing without any support or validation. This is much like breaking your arm and your leg, but only putting a cast on your leg and letting the arm heal as best it can.

The overall concept of creating your shame-proof village is to stop thinking that your parent identity is the only piece that can be supported—and stop thinking that the only support you can accept is from people who are also parents.

Yes, you have less time because of your children. But they are watching you be a human. They are learning about relationships, communication, goal setting, success, failure, and developing an identity from you. Don't stop getting support from each aspect of who you are—especially the parts that you closely and passionately identify with—and create a shame-proof village that not only supports your parenting, but one that supports you as a whole human.

Friendship

The foundation of your shame-proof village is to create a support system of people, places, and resources that provide an empathetic space for you to grow, learn, reflect, guide, and be yourself. The catch here is this: your shame-proof village is something you've already learned how to create.

It's called friendship.

Ha. I kind of got you on that one. The idea of a shame-proof village for parents, though, is that you don't give up aspects of your identity because you are a parent. You don't give up the friendships you once had because they don't have kids yet. You don't stop enjoying the things you once enjoyed because you can only focus on your kids now. The shame-proofing of your support means that you still get to use the human support you had before you had kids, and bring it into your new role as a parent.

This means that you take the shame-proof parenting framework, and let those you want in your shame-proof village know more about this new piece of your identity.

Let's move away from your parenting for a second. As you've grown into your adult life, you've had people come and go. But the ones who remained were the ones who continued to understand that your growth didn't hinder their growth. When conflicts arose, you handled them with maturity and communication. When you made a mistake, they offered a listening ear to help you get through it. And even if they didn't fully understand your current ideas and thoughts, they were there for you. This is how you created lifelong friendships.

The same process occurs once you become a parent. Becoming a parent is a growing moment in your life. Just as you reassessed friends after a major promotion or a relationship change, you can do the same once you have kids. Allow your current friends to show you that they can still support you, even if it's just to offer you a glass of wine and a seat on their couch to vent. The idea here is to reassess, not just assume that your friends will change how they respond to you once you become a parent.

Seek out non-parents

Too many times I see parents fall into the myth that only other parents understand them. They believe that unless you're a parent who has lived through what they've lived through, you can't possibly understand what it means to raise a human.

But here's where parents feed into the shame that our culture has created for them. When you believe that you can learn nothing from someone unless they have lived the exact same life as you, you're cutting yourself off from real growth. And in turn, you're stopping yourself from possibly creating a village of support that will not only commiserate with you, but can also challenge you and push you out of your comfort zone.

Growth is just on the other end of your comfort zone. This is true when you are building a business, trying to make any significant change, or attempting to do things that no one else is doing. And if you think of all the self-help inspirational quotes that we share online, the main theme is that when you refuse to grow, learn, or reflect, you remain stagnant in the same spot. The stubbornness we hold onto will always keep us stagnant. If you believe this, then you have most likely made some amazing changes in your life that have helped you move forward in a positive way.

Thus, as a parent, if you only stay around people who think the same, are going through the same tough situations, and most likely are having the same emotions that you're having, you will stay stuck. And non-parents can give you exactly the perspective you need on life, even when you don't want to hear it. The key here is not to let everyone in your space, but to be open if someone who doesn't have kids wants to share with you. In this space you hear them, and they hear you out, and you can come to a conclusion that allows you to make the final choice for your parenting identity. If the non-parent is not able to have this transaction, that's okay. Just don't allow that one non-parent interaction to sour your perspective on everyone who is not a parent yet.

Seek out parents

This happens almost naturally. Parents, especially parents who have children the same age, look for each other at playgrounds and parties. It's good for your soul to commiserate and realize that you are not alone in your struggle. It's nice to know that you're not the only parent who hasn't slept and who is second guessing everything. These connections are great for managing the guilt and shame that come up for you when you sit at home feeling like a failure. I encourage support groups and I also encourage you to find ones that support you in ways that make you feel whole (i.e., don't just go to the newest, hottest parenting support group because you think you should). For shame-proofing your parenting, think about both where you feel the most at home and where you think you'll have space to be honest about your parenting experiences. You don't want to be stuck in a parenting support group that only wants to hear how things are going well; you want to be able to talk about the messiness of being a parent too. If you can't share that you made mac and cheese seven days in a row without feeling shamed, then that is not the parenting support group for you. If you need some ideas of where you can find parenting support groups, here are a few ideas:

Your Child's School: Start by asking your child's local school about parent volunteer opportunities. Many schools have a parent center where parents come to help the school with events and morale. That's right, Parent. You thought the parent center was a place where the school elicits free labor out of you. But essentially, it's a great place to find other parents to share experience with and gain support.

The Local Library: The local library has a lot of activities for you and your child to enjoy. However, they always have congenial ways for parents to join together to support each other, such as a book club or parenting class. You'd also be surprised how easy it is to meet other parents at the library and begin a support network for yourself right in your neighborhood. Next time you're there to get books with your kid, look at the events board to see if they offer any activities for parents.

Community Centers: This is a more obvious venue because many community centers post flyers in the community about parent support groups. This is the best place to find groups that are more geared towards specific types of parent support, such as single parenting, co-parenting, or parenting groups in different languages. It's also a place where you can find activities to share with your children and continue to build that ever-important relationship with them.

Health Clinics and Non-Profits Agencies: This might be the least liked idea for joining a parent support group. Most parents link these places with mental health issues and stigmatize the help and services the agencies provide. But these places have funding to make extraordinary support groups for parents. They often offer parent training and therapeutic interventions by skilled professionals. Also, they're more likely to have food at the meeting because they have a small amount of funds to do this, which is always a great thing. The best thing is that you can get professional assistance with mental health and behavioral issues that you are experiencing with your child.

And, in the event that you cannot find any authentic group that supports your unique parenting journey, then:

Create Your Own Shame-Proof Parenting Group: If none of the spaces listed here float your boat, then you can create your own! Sometimes you can even create this group at one of the venues listed above. The idea behind creating your own is that you take the reigns of the meeting and make it what you want: informal, informational, or just a venting session. You can also develop strong friendships with other parents whom you can access in times of need, or just to watch your kids for a few hours.

Sometimes you just have to remind yourself that
you don't have to do what everyone else is doing.

—Unknown

Be wary of social media

Even though social media is a great place to stay connected to all sorts
of people, be wary of how much you rely on social media for your
relationships. I talk to countless parents who tell me that it is so hard to
parent these days because of social media. There is this constant need to
compare yourself to other families. Even though you have enough sense
to know that these parents are probably going through the same level of
mess as you, it's hard to remember that when they post pictures of their
family at the zoo or amusement park, and you're stuck at home for the
100th weekend in a row because your child has a tendency to act out
when in public.

One mom explained to me that she has to sometimes unfollow her friends
because the pictures are too much. But it's not even the posts that get to
parents. Sometimes it's the Pinterest level preparations that some parents
share. Not all parents are able to—or even want to—do these types of
parties or events. But for some reason, even the parents who don't want
to do this have a hard time separating themselves from shame and guilt
over not giving their child a huge party.

I think that of all the stories relating to social media I've heard, the one
that affected me the most was one mom who shared with me that she
felt shamed by parents in her community, because of what she *wasn't*
posting on social media. This mom stated that she never thought she'd
be shamed because she didn't post all her family's vacations and events
online. She stated that she was never into sharing online, even when she
was single. So, it didn't occur to her to do it once she was married and
had a family. She shared that when her children got to elementary school

and she began to accept friend requests from the parents of the kids in her children's class, she felt the sting of comparison rear its ugly head, which is why she was so opposed to being on social media in the first place. But the parents in her child's class said that they post a lot about the school and events in the community on social media, so she should be on, at least Facebook, more. So, she did. After a few months of posting things here and there, she was shamed at a parent meeting by a group of parents for not posting enough. The shaming wasn't done blatantly; it was more subtle. The "oh we don't even know what you guys do on the weekends since you don't post at all" kind of comments were what stung the most. The other parents all talked about sharing pictures so that they could connect with family and friends who weren't able to see their children regularly. But when this mom explained that she actually takes pictures and shares them via email with the people she wanted to see them, the other parents laughed at her for this. So, she felt horrible.

After that incident, she started posting more and sharing more, but that she felt as if she had been forced into doing so, and for a while she did it begrudgingly. When she stumbled upon my end parent shaming posts and found one that said she didn't have to do what others parents were doing to be a good parent, she felt relieved. She stated that this post gave her the confidence she needed to stop posting so much if she didn't want to, and to ignore the moms who made snide comments about it. She even started interacting with other moms like her who didn't care about social media as much and she felt better knowing that she did not have to be like everyone else.

Step-by-step to creating your shame-proof village

1. Identify what you're passionate about: The things that you are passionate about make-up who you are. We find our passions from how we see the world and how we interact with the world. Passions are not solely hobbies or things that we do well; they also encompass dreams, things we love, and things that bring

us happiness. When you are creating your shame-proof village, you want to be honest about what makes you feel happy and passionate. Everyone has something that they are passionate about, even if you've never said it out loud because it feels silly or you think people will laugh at you. The interesting thing is that you cannot ignore the things that bring you happiness—even if you haven't taken part in them for a while.

2. Think about who you want in your corner: This includes anyone who you have been around or who you want to be around, who has ever made you feel good about yourself. I often ask my parents to write a list of people they love or would love to be around—including celebrities or well-known people. I then ask them to detail what traits or aspects of these people's identities they admire. Armed with that information, they can go out into the world to find people (or find groups online) that embody these aspects. I encourage you to try this exercise too.

3. Describe what type of space you need: I'm talking about space in terms of support and feeling safe. I've talked about creating this space for your child. But when it comes to what you need to feel safe, to open up and be honest about your whole human experience, take time to think about what it is that you really need. For example, I used to attend a group for foster and adoptive parents who shared that they loved this space, because as adoptive and foster parents, they felt that they could talk about the unique dynamics that come up for them that do not come up for biological families.

4. Assess your strengths and weaknesses: As I've stated earlier in the book, your strengths will help you feel confident, but your weaknesses will show you where you need support. In addressing them while creating your shame-proof village, you can find support to high-five you when you succeed and excel in

your strengths, but also support you and give you space to grow in your weaknesses. It's something that you have in your friends, and you can bring it to your shame-proof parenting village, too.

5. Be consistently reflective, and lean into change: The support you needed with a newborn is going to be different than the support you need with a tween, so get comfortable with reassessing your village as you and your children grow. People come and go, and as they do, reflect on what they left you with, what they took from you, and reassess how that helped you grow. I remember wanting to leave my second-year internship because I hated my supervisor in grad school, so I called my wonderful supervisor from first year, ready to quit. She told me that if I learned nothing else from this supervisor, I would learn what not to do. This truth can be expanded to creating your shame-proof village: no matter how long or how short a person stays in your village, remember that they will teach you something about who you are and about a piece of your identity that will inevitably seep into your parenting. Leaning into this change, and all the emotions that come with it, will help you make peace with yourself, and in turn help you be more empathetic to your child's development, and their humanness.

Conclusion

Getting support and finding the kind of support that celebrates the whole you is not rocket science. We all know that when we have support we do things a hundred times better than when we do it on our own. The part that created a barrier is the shame that can come with exposing ourselves to others. When we share who we are and what we're experiencing, we leave ourselves open to critique and judgment. This is why it is so important to create your shame-proof village: a village of support that does not take advantage of your vulnerability and one where being a whole human is just as important as being a parent. The idea is that no matter how introverted or extroverted you are, when you take control of the type of support you need, you get to create a shame-proof parenting village that supports the whole you—and your family can benefit from that level of all-encompassing, empathetic, loving support!

But I know that creating a shame-proof village isn't equally as easy for everyone. If you already feel like something of an outcast because of race, religion, sexuality, or some other core piece of your identity, how can you navigate this task of both shame-proofing your parenting and gathering a supportive village around you? That's exactly what we're diving into next.

BURSTING THE SHAME-PROOF PARENTING BUBBLE

Don't make up stories about your ability or self-worth based on totally flawed information.

—Denise Duffield Thomas

As an African-American woman, I can't tell you how many times I've read something in the self-help section of the bookstore and thought, "They're not really talking to me." I think it was also something that I realized in my undergraduate and graduate study as I learned about psychological issues, interventions, and theories. What I realized is that many of the behavioral and psychological studies ignored the people I identified with. And while I know that many studies can be extrapolated to include other groups of people, the exclusion of minority groups as part of the main research makes it harder to see myself in the results and in these interventions.

In parenting, I've seen the same thing occur many times. Beyond anything that separates us, I realize that a lot of the voices and perspectives seem to be one sided. Maybe it's because I don't always look for it (the different voices, the inclusiveness), but maybe it's also because it's not there. When you think about the various cultures and groups of people that raise children, we have to realize that the mainstream White American Way is not the only way. Nor is it the best.

The Western culture of parenting sometimes misses the mark when it comes to how others come into their parenting identity, and we must ask ourselves how much of that discovery is done in the context of how that person identifies culturally, racially, sexually, and by gender. In one of my favorite discussions on parenting, author Alfie Kohn explains that "over and over, what we take to be simple facts about child development turn out not to be true everywhere."[16] And in that statement, we have to be aware that even though this book is aimed at developing a parenting identity in a Western culture, there is still a lot of diversity that we often fail to account for in our parenting culture.

So many of the topics we take for granted and grasp at for validation take on a whole other meaning when you think of the diversity in how we all identify. I think about more communal cultures, where there is a sense of togetherness and closeness that is not always valued in our individualistic Western culture. In communal identities, the need to be autonomous is not as highly valued as the goal of togetherness and taking care of one another; nor is the idea that unconditional love or acceptance is even an issue, because it implies a universal understanding of individualistic ideals.[17] Another example in my research showed that we often assume that everyone has access to the same resources and financial means, which can manifest in parents placing more value on rules and discipline that are related to how that parent is treated in society and their perspective on the world.[18] When we ignore these differences in how a human can develop their parenting identity, we leave that parent open to more instances of shame in trying to conform to what Western society has deemed appropriate and right.

In this often unconscious dismissal, we miss the ideas that help families feel more connected to one another and not so isolated. I can attest to the fact that we have gotten very far away from communal living and have moved more toward the individual thinking of our Western society.

---

16   Kohn, A. Unconditional parenting: Moving from rewards and punishments to love and reason, 2005. New York, NY, United States: Atria Books.

17   Rothbaum, F., & Trommsdorff, G. "Do roots and wings complement or oppose one another?: The socialization of relatedness and autonomy in cultural context." In Handbook of socialization: Theory and research (1st ed.), 2006. New York: Guilford Publications.

18   Kohn, M. Class and conformity: A study in values (2nd ed.), 1977. Chicago: University of Chicago Press.

The more research we do, the more we realize how bad it is to raise children without community. But despite this movement toward more individual child-raising, we cannot ignore the fact that there are many factors that lead a parent to develop their parenting identity, which have more to do with the cultural ideals they have embedded in their minds than the biggest societal perspectives. One example of this is illustrated in ideas about discipline and corporal punishment. While many current parenting strategies condemn the practice, you'd be surprised to know that even now almost "80% of parents around the world spank their children."[19] Even with all the research against spanking that details the long-term consequences of this type of punishment, we still have a society that believes that this method of discipline is acceptable and useful.

But here's the deal: I am not saying that culture determines whether someone will use spanking or not, or whether a parent will allow their child to be more independent or not. What I am saying is that we have to be mindful of how the cultural framework in which a parent develops their parenting identity influences their child-rearing practices, and instead of demonizing them, shaming them, or even throwing research their way, we have to stop and empathize, get to know them, and support these parents so they can see how various perspectives will help them raise healthy children. We can no longer assume that everyone thinks the same and will assimilate to one way of thinking. That's the essence of shame in my opinion: measuring each other based on a biased and one-sided measuring stick.

On that same note, I further believe that the closer we get to reaching the mainstream White American goal of perfect parenting, the more we ignore the richness that community and support can offer us. If we constantly ignore who we are, how we came to be who we are, and allow this disconnect to build up shame in us, we will eventually create

---

19   Grogan-Kaylor, A. & Gershoff, E. Spanking and child outcomes: Old controversies and new meta-analyses. Journal of Family Psychology, 30(4), 453-469, 2016. http://dx.doi.org/10.1037/fam0000191

a parenting culture devoid of any variation and authenticity. And no matter how much you want to argue that, I think we all know that when we dismiss an aspect of someone's identity—especially their cultural identity—we essentially lose that person and any effort to support them in making healthier choices.

Additionally, we must get rid of the myth that you shouldn't have to read a book or get support for your parenting, which is one thing that I am trying to dispel in this book. The current parenting movement comes from the mainstream America idea of being able to have all your resources, being able to have all the support, being able to have access and be treated with the same faculties as everybody else; and sometimes that's just not apparent. How do we bridge the gap between what we have come to understand in the research that comes from Western science, and what a person's cultural understanding of the world brings to their parenting identity? The labels we've created in our Western society don't always resonate outside that context, and can sometimes be seen as offensive to the more communal aspects of someone's culture. Again, when we get better at providing a space for healthy discussions on child-rearing practices—and not hide behind the safety of research—we can actually find ways to get through to one another across cultural lines.

Also, if we break it down into cultural influences on parenting that span past race, we can see that culture is all the nuanced and complicated things that truly makes us who we are as humans, before we are even parents. When we ignore or dismiss these features, it becomes very difficult to shame-proof your parenting, because you find yourself trying to fit into a brand of parenting that does not encompass your whole self, but rather another self that you may not fully identify with. Confidence in your parenting comes from embracing the imperfections of who you are, and that includes all of your identities: cultural, sexual, economic, and gender identity. Just as you can't let go of your whole identity when you become a parent, you also can't ignore how your culture affects you.

Within this discussion, let's explore what shame-proofing looks like when you don't fit the stereotypical profile as a parent.

Cultural influences

Cultural influences are the most important aspect of shame-proofing your parenting and protecting your family from shame. Why? It's because no matter how Americanized you are, you cannot escape the culture you identify with—even if you can "pass" for another culture. Even when you try to assimilate into the mainstream culture, your family, friends, and community all encompass how you see yourself and how your children will come to see themselves.

Reflect on what child-rearing looks like in your culture. For example, in my African-American culture, there are child-rearing ideas that include a child obeying and an adult having authority, as well as using corporal punishment to discipline a child. While not every person in this culture believes in this or participates in these behaviors, it is a part of my African-American child-raising history that will influence the ways in which I go about raising a child of my own. There's no denying that. The interesting thing about this is that many cultures have child-rearing practices that you may want to shy away from or you might think are outdated. However, reflective processing on these practices helps you to shame-proof your parenting in a way that allows you to make choices based on why and not just a judgment on your culture's ideology. When you know why you are choosing against or moving towards a parenting strategy, it helps you protect your parenting identity and your family, because you're not going to be easily offended and/or pulled astray. You know why you're making this decision, and you feel grounded, as opposed to feeling defensive.

But even further than racial identity, there are other aspects of culture that come out in how we raise children. How children are respected, how parents are supported, who gets authority over your children, what a child is allowed to know, what holidays you celebrate, annual events you participate in, the foods you eat or are allowed to eat, the way you are supposed to dress, etc. All these ideas and more are embedded in your cultural understanding of how you see yourself as you grew up and how you raise your children. It can be difficult to change patterns when you refuse to at least reflect on the positives and negatives of your cultural identity. It can also be difficult to change your own parenting strategies if you're not aware of how culturally bound they are. This fact is why I encourage you to look at your parenting through a cultural lens and not just assimilate to another parenting expert's ideas. (Yes, I'm also talking about mine, too.) This is because much of our child-raising practices come from some cultural foundation, whether we know it or not.

Gender identity/sexual orientation

A lot is said about being the parent of a child who has come out, but very few things are said about the shame around being a parent who is in the LGBTQIA community. When I worked in a foster/adoption agency, I worked with a few families who identified in the LGBTQIA community. One of the biggest issues that came up for these parents was having to face a world that still had biases and judgments against them. The children who were adopted never minded that they had two moms or two dads. But what these children did report was getting questions about why this was or being teased because of it. And that is the shame that we sometimes ignore for families that identify in this culture.

Part of shame-proofing your parenting within this community is to acknowledge that if you are living with biases, so are your children. As I'm sure you're aware, if you identify in this community, we are still a world that does not know how to manage differences well. And if your children do not identify in this community, I encourage you to do more than just protect them from the cruelness of the world. I encourage you to use the shame-proof strategies that we have talked about here to help your children learn more about who they are, how they identify, and to get comfortable about diversity. Again, shame-proofing your family does not mean that you will not be met with adversity or bypass conflict; but it does give your family a foundation to manage external conflict in a way that helps you grow together.

Religious/spiritual influences

I was raised in a religious home where we went to church, read the bible, and worshipped the Christian God. This was a foundation that played a huge part in how I identified myself. The Christian faith has commentary on how children are to be raised, and my family was huge on following those ideals. And while I have grown up to find my own spiritual path that does not solely include the Christian God, I think that the foundation I received as a child has supported my spiritual journey, in both good and bad ways. I share this because religion and spirituality is one of the common topics that I discuss with parents, mostly because many parents have the same story I just shared—they grew up in a religious home.

What I see more commonly is parents wanting their children to believe the same faith or spiritual truths that they believe in. The good news is that if you're truly interested in shame-proofing your family, there is a way to incorporate spiritual beliefs and religion, and that's by living the way your religion asks you to live and by growing your spiritual identity in healthy ways. This may seem like a no-brainer for the parent who has a religious identity, but it is oftentimes difficult to model that religion for your child while you are still on your own spiritual journey. Even for the most devout parent, being open and honest about your religious/spiritual journey will actually encourage your child to start—and even maintain—that sense of spiritual curiosity that will help them forge their own religious/spiritual insights. Here is an empowering suggestion for walking a more honest spiritual practice for your shame-proof parenting: reflect on your spirituality, including the parts that you love, the parts that you're not sure of, the pieces that you question, and the pieces that you'd like to grow in. In essence, the more honest and human you are about the journey of being a religious/spiritual being, the more your child will be able to decide if they want to incorporate it into their lives.

When we force it on our children, they begin to associate religion/ spirituality with punishment, boredom, and negativity. Additionally, when our children see you living in a way that contradicts your religion/ spirituality, they begin to turn from it because of that hypocrisy. It is that truth that leads me to encourage parents to be honest about the difficulty you experience trying to live as your religion tells you to, and give your child space to be imperfect in their religious growth, as well.

Essentially, what I love about using religion/spirituality to shame-proof your parenting, is that it gives you another layer of support that you and your family can use when tensions run high and conflict feels too intense. But the way to make it a tool in your family, as opposed to another source of contention, is to be open to how you interpret and use your religion, as well as how your children begin to embrace or reject it. It can be tough to allow this, but in doing so you give yourself space to be a human—not a perfect religious follower—and you give your child space to find what helps them feel fulfilled in their spiritual journey.

Media portrayals of parenting

As I was researching this book, I found a whole page on parenting tropes in television/movies. It was at the site, TVTropes.org, a site that compiles all the tropes and motifs that we find in movies and television. What struck me as interesting was how many tropes we have come to know and understand—everything from the Doting Parent trope who believes her children are the best, to the Overprotective Dad trope used mostly in comedies, who won't let his daughter go out with the bad-boy boyfriend. And although these tropes are based in reality, they can neglect one simple thing: most parents are a hodgepodge of all these types of characters. This is a truth that I think many of the parents I work with forget as well. While we all use entertainment as a way to project ourselves and our problems, we sometimes forget that the characters and situations we're watching were crafted by writers and filmed by directors. Of course, the parents get it right—or mess it up with a laugh track.

Instead of judging yourself by the impossible standards of these parenting tropes in isolation, try watching these characters with a shame-proof parenting lens. Watch a show with your family, and each of you dissect which of you is which character and how your family would have managed that situation. This way you can allow the media portrayals to be a source of growth for you and your family, as opposed to allowing these impossible ideals to plague your thinking and shame you into thinking that you are less-than as a parent.

One family that I worked with used this strategy as both a time to bond with each other, and a way for the parent to find out how their children were processing issues in the world. This family watched a comedy show called *Blackish*. The family not only identified with the family in the show, but they also used the show to talk about important issues that arose for the fictional family members. As this family watched episodes about sibling rivalry and parental disagreements on discipline, the family I was working with was able to use those fictional situations to problem solve the same issues in their family.

I remember during one session, the mom was having a difficult time listening to her son about an altercation he had at school. As the son was attempting to explain what happened and watching his mom get frustrated, I asked him if any of the characters on Blackish had dealt with this. It was like a light bulb went off in his head, and he began to detail an episode where the daughter on the show had to deal with a group of mean girls, and he was able to link his behaviors and the altercation to that episode. Not only did the mom finally understand, but she was able to remind him of how the parents helped the daughter in the show and how the daughter resolved the issue. In that moment, the *Pleasantville* solution from the show actually helped this family find the solution for their real life issue without causing the tension and conflict they were used to.

I would further challenge you to create a list of the traits that you love in the parenting tropes you find yourself gravitating towards, and to do the same for the ones that turn you off and that you avoid. Then do some reflective parenting so that you can see how they either already show up in your life, or how you'd like them to.

Don't allow those tropes to consume and overwhelm you as you attempt to shame-proof your parenting. Remember your parenting journey will look different than anyone else's, simply because you are a unique human, and remember that those parents in media that you're comparing yourself to are all fictional people who have the words written for them and the solutions to problems solved for them already!

Conclusion

In the shame-proof parenting framework, it's not simply a matter of acknowledging how our larger cultural ideals influence us, but it's really about getting reflective and figuring out how both large and small influences factor into how you develop your parenting identity. It can be easy to ignore, shun, or even demonize the aspects of our culture that make us feel icky. But as we've talked about in this framework: you can't shame-proof something you have no idea is at work in your parenting. Being able to look at your cultural identity, your sexual identity, and your gender identity—even if it all falls under the mainstream—in a reflective and honest way, will not only help you build empathy for yourself when you go astray, it will model for your child how to do the same. The last thing any parent wants is for their child to ignore and hate aspects of their identity.

WHEN ALL THE PIECES OF SHAME-PROOF PARENTING COME TOGETHER

Our job is not to deny the story, but to defy the ending—to rise strong, recognize our story, and rumble with the truth until we get to a place where we think: Yes. This is what happened. This is my truth and I will choose how this story ends.

—*Brené Brown*

One day about six years ago, I had had enough. The funny thing was that it was just a normal phone call, about what we were going to do for Mother's Day. As she refused to change the venue because it was "her" day, and I was still reeling from altercations with her daughters and not wanting to be around them, we both lost each other. But in that seemingly innocuous phone call, I had reached my limit with a mother who didn't seem to see anyone other than herself. Without a lot of fanfare, I decided at the end of the call to stop talking to her. I remember feeling sick to my stomach and knowing that I was making a huge decision. The years of trying to be a perfect daughter, mixed with the years of trying to understand her through my psychology schooling, combined with the heartache of knowing that she'd never truly be the biological mother that left me, was finally too much to bear. And the sad thing is that at the end of the call, she didn't even know that I was making that decision.

You might say that this decision started me on the path to shame-proof parenting. I didn't know it then, of course, but what I realized now—since hindsight is 20/20 after all—is that our relationship was not shame-proof at all. I mean, duh, right? But my point is to show you that neither of us knew how to manage conflict; we were both interacting with each other through old wounds and a barrier of walls. We were both operating as if the other was the enemy, and we were both lost in ignoring our humanness for the sake of showing off for our community and family (me being the perfect daughter and her being the best mother ever).

And while I seriously thought about how we could continue being in a relationship—even if distant—I knew that I needed to disconnect from that relationship if I was going to heal and move into a healthier phase of my life. For me, the shame-proofing of our relationship came in me finding the courage to choose my sanity over her. And if that sounds harsh, I am shame-proofed enough to withstand your critique. In essence, in order to get back to my imperfect, authentic humanness, I had to untie myself from the fantasy of what my mother needed me to be. And, if I want to make an educated guess, I've allowed her to do the same for her own identity (but, since I still don't talk to her, I can't say what's she really doing).

But you won't get any preaching or a cautionary tale from me. What you get from this reflection of my own relationship is that shaming and living with the weight of that shame, is enough to make disconnection an unfortunate but sometimes necessary solution.

Now, that doesn't seem like a very nice tie up of all that I've walked you through during the course of this book. But, in fact, it really is!

Shame-proof parenting is not about getting it right; rather, it's about being comfortable in the fluidity of our humanness. We desperately want to raise perfect children who don't have the same flaws as us, but in doing so we create a space that is impossible to actually breathe in, for yourself or for your child. I know that it can be difficult to look at your child and not see your own failures when they don't measure up to expectations, but the good news is that you get to set the expectation bar. This bar is set by your own reflective process, and you can set it at a level where you and your child can healthily create a relationship based on connection and empathy. In this framework, you don't worry about being too lenient or too permissive. Instead, you focus more on the process of being fluidly human—the successful bits, the flawed bits, and all that's in between.

As I was wrapping up this book, I came across an article posted on social media about supporting teens through not getting the gift they wanted for the holidays. The article talked about strategies that parents could use to give their teen space to deal with disappointment and frustration, which are strategies I often share with my parents. But when I checked out the comments, many of them worried that giving empathy in this situation would make a child an asshole. As I read the comments, it got me thinking about the shame-proof parenting framework and how we tend to link feelings and emotional literacy with leniency and permissiveness, and that can make giving space for feelings a negative image that no one wants to be associated with.

I feel that this happens in a world that believes that being tough is about managing the behaviors and not giving space to the motivations that drive the behaviors. This can happen when we've been taught—mostly indirectly—that there is a set time and place for feelings. We grow to learn that feelings have to be controlled in order for us to be decent humans. The side effect of this perspective is often maladaptive behavior. But because we're so detached from our feelings, being able to see that link can often be impossible.

It's in this notion that I believe shame-proof parenting can really change the way we look at parents. In creating a space for you to be more authentic, you create humans who are more authentic, and in turn produce a society of people who understand that you need both logical strategies and emotional support to be fully human. This may feel hokey, but when you think of the journey you've taken throughout this book, you now know that being a shame-proof parent helps create that emotional literacy for both you and your child, and sets you both up to cope with the ebbs and flows of being a human in this world.

Shifting the blaming paradigm in parenting

As I peruse the parenting section on Amazon, I am struck by how many books blame the parents. In my head, as I read description after description of how parents are overprotective, overbearing, trying too hard, being too materialistic, or wanting their kid to succeed too much, I couldn't help but think—does anyone see a pattern here?

We've become a culture of critique that feels the need to tell parents that striving to make the best out of who you care for is a flaw that should be punished with judgment and shame. We've done this without looking at our own selves and without realizing the biggest common issue here: parents don't forfeit their humanness once they take on the role of raising kids.

They still feel. They still think. They still have character flaws. They still make mistakes. They still have goals and dreams. They still have successes. And all of this does not have to be tied to their parenting identity.

We somehow got it mixed up somewhere down the line that becoming a parent (biologically or not) gives humans a superpower. And while some of you who read this book will promptly throw it down (or delete it from your device) on the premise that no one is going to tell you that you're not superhuman for raising kids, I'll calmly ask you to think of the burden of that thought and the pressure of society that comes with it!

Superheroes and people with superhuman abilities have a huge burden: they've got to save a world that doesn't know it needs saving. They've got to anticipate crime and bad guys so they can stop them before anyone gets hurt. And when they don't? The guilt and shame is enough to crush them—only it doesn't because you know, they've got Kryptonian blood coursing through their veins.

There are times you get the approval of others for rocking it. But, more often than not, you're crushed under the impossible expectations placed on you to raise a healthy human being, while sometimes not being the healthiest human yourself.

And again, there might be a sentiment of: Yeah, I feel that weight everyday and I'm still standing. But when we look at the current state of parenting, it's been said that raising kids is more burdensome than losing your spouse or losing a job![20] To me, that's not *still standing*; that's barely hanging on.

The shame-proof framework gets us back to what it means to be a human raising another human, and gets us to stop glorifying the notion that we need to be superhuman to raise a kid.

If I had one wish for my professional path, it would be to create a shame-proof world for parents to find a healthy identity and raise healthy humans. I say shame-proof because it's not about being shame *free*, but more about learning how to withstand shame so it doesn't infiltrate the relationship parents have with themselves and their children!

My hope for you and your family under the shame-proof framework is that you don't have to disconnect from one another, as I did, to be healthy, but that you can find this healthfulness and safety in your family.

And with that goal, I want to leave you with this reminder as you start your shame-proof parenting journey:

---

20   Cha, A. It turns out parenthood is worse than divorce, unemployment — even the death of a partner. The Washington Post, 2015. Retrieved from https:// www.washingtonpost.com/news/to-your-health/wp/2015/08/11/the-most-depressing-statistic-imaginable-about-being-a-new-parent/?utm_term=.4d10e0c8b806

Being wholly, authentically human is a lifelong journey that no one ever truly masters. Give yourself space to be imperfect, and make a commitment to shame-proof your parenting identity, so that you can give that same space to your children.

CONNECT WITH THE AUTHOR

If you're looking for help in your parenting journey, I would be honored to connect with you and invite you into a supportive community, a true shame-proof village of parents, who are all doing their best to raise whole, healthy children.

You can find out more about me and shame-proof parenting here:

Website: http://shameproofparenting.com

Facebook: http://www.facebook.com/ShameProofParenting

Twitter: http://www.twitter.com/ParentSkillz

Instagram: http://www.instagram.com/ShameProofParenting

LinkedIn: http://www.linkedin.com/in/MercedesSamudioLCSW

And as you implement the philosophies and strategies I've described for you in this book, I would love it if you could post your experiences on social media and use the hashtag #EndParentShaming.

For downloadable versions of the worksheets, templates, and figures in the book, please visit: https://shameproofparenting.com/shameproofparentingextras/

ACKNOWLEDGEMENTS

"Acknowledging the good that you already have in your life is the foundation for all abundance."

-Eckart Tolle

Writing a book is a long journey and a transformative process. While the words you've read in this book are from me, the path to getting them on the page and to you was not solely me.

I am so grateful for the team at Paper Raven Books. Morgan, you are a rock star. You told me I'd have a book in three months—and I had a book in three months. Thank you for your encouragement, for your rocking organizational skills, and most of all, for believing in me and my message. To my amazing editors, you both taught me a lot about my tolerance levels for getting my work critiqued and made me grow as a writer because of it. To the rest of the team behind the scenes, thank you for helping me bring my message into the world.

To my husband who supported me throughout the process, who became my thesaurus when I was searching for another way to make a point, listening to me rant on and on about how I want to change the world, and challenging me to make my message more succinct. Because of you, I will be the Oprah of the parenting world!

To the parents who allowed me to be a part of their parenting journey and gave me permission to use their stories, thank you. I feel so blessed to be a part of your journeys, and I hope that your stories will empower and encourage other families to stand up against parenting shame.

To my beta readers, thank you for taking the time out of your busy schedules to read the book and offer insights. You will never know how much that meant to me and I hope that you know that I am forever grateful to you and your encouragement.

To everyone who's followed me on my #endparentshaming journey, thank you from the bottom of my heart. You helped turn a thought into a movement, and showed me that it is still possible to change the world. I hope this book makes you proud to be a part of this movement.